deathly still

Dirk Reinartz
Christian Graf von Krockow

deathly still

Translated from the German
by Ishbel Flett

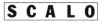

Contents

Foreword   The time of the concentration camps began almost as soon as the Nazis came to power in Germany in 1933, after Hitler had been appointed Chancellor and sworn to uphold the democratic constitution of the Weimar Republic. It lasted until April or early May 1945, when the final remaining camps were liberated by Allied troops. Since then, half a century has passed. Survivors, victims and perpetrators alike, have already died, or are nearing the end of their three score years and ten. What was once the present has now become history. Just as we glean our impressions today at second and even at third hand – from books, from documentaries, or from such films as *Schindler's List* – so too are we now creating memorials of a new and different kind, in places far from the scene of the crime, in Washington, D.C. or in Frankfurt am Main.

They still exist, of course, the places where the concentration camps stood. They, too, have become memorials. But so often they invite the rhetoric of pathos, pandering to the gruesome curiosity of horror tourism, complete with chattering guides and a brisk trade in souvenirs equal to any medieval fortress with its dungeons and torture chambers.

What can we learn here? Little enough, one might imagine. Only with many patient hours of meditation can we absorb what we see, can these impressions take effect, can such silence find a voice. But opening hours are restricted. Just one quick snapshot! The guides want to go home. The visitors are already headed for the next stop on their tour. After Dachau, they can enjoy the convivial atmosphere of a traditional Munich *biergarten:* The perfect antidote. But this is, after all, human nature, and who are we to scorn?

Patience and meditation. Perhaps a book like this can help. For it is with patience and with much care that these pictures have been collected over the years throughout Germany and Europe; collected wherever there were concentration camps, wherever there were factories of death.

Order and isolation The first thing we see is the double iron gateway emblazoned with the claim *Arbeit macht frei* (Work makes free), or *Jedem das Seine* (To each his own). The first is an unequivocal reminder that all who pass through the gates have lost their freedom, though, just possibly, it may be won back by effort. The second is the time-honoured motto of the Prussian monarchy, taken from the Latin, *suum quique,* a declaration of justice promising each his due according to his status and achievement. On the gates of a concentration camp, it mocks all who enter, as if deserving of their fate.

Except for the central turret over the entrance, the buildings are plain, solid, austere. This is no place for dreams. Within these walls, behind these windows, is a world of files and registers where clerks and minor officials administer their regime of paper-stamping and form-filling and list-making, defending that very sense of order without which everything would collapse into anarchy. If there was ever any truth in the claim that the Germans loved order and feared chaos more than any other people, then surely the proof is here.

This love of order permeates every camp. Of course, in many cases, much of the evidence has been destroyed. Wherever the Germans had time, they blew up or burnt what they could – especially files – before the Allied troops arrived. In Bergen–Belsen, British troops burned down the barracks to check the spread of disease. Many camps were in use again soon afterwards as PoW or refugee camps. Then, sooner or later, they were partly or wholly reconstructed as memorials with, in some cases, aesthetic considerations taking precedence over authenticity. A few of the camps were closed down at an early stage and never reopened, as in Emsland in 1936. To look there for traces now would be bordering on the archaeological.

As a rule, however, the basic outline of the constructions are still clearly recognisable. Nowhere is there an irregular detail the eye might rest upon. The boundary lines are straight and true, drawn in a precise rectangle or, as in Sachsenhausen, in the form of an equilateral triangle. Then, as now, the barracks lined the alleys and crescents with mathematical precision. And, of course, wherever they went in the camps, to and from work, prisoners had to march in step, filing in to assemble for roll-call.

The second thing we feel is the sense of isolation, and, at the same time, the understanding of its opposite. In so many ways in these camps, isolation was non-existent: no bush or tree, no quiet corner where one might be alone or meet discreetly; no locker where one might stow anything personal; no chance of retaining a keepsake, a letter or a photograph. The bed is a symbol of privacy. This may explain why, of all things, the bed – still to be seen in some of the barracks – was to become the focus of an almost hysterical public attentiveness. As Primo Levi describes it:

"… making beds (*Bettenbauen*: this was the technical term) was a sacral operation to be performed in accordance with iron rules … For the SS in the camp, and consequently for all barracks heads, *Bettenbauen* had a prime and indecipherable importance: perhaps it was a symbol of order and discipline. Anyone who did not make his bed properly, or forgot to make it, was punished publicly and savagely; furthermore, in every barracks there existed a pair of functionaries, the *Bettnachzieher* ('bed after-pullers': a term that I do not believe exists in normal German and that Goethe certainly would not have understood) whose task it was to check every single bed and then take care of its transversal alignment. For this purpose, they were equipped with a string the length of the hut: they stretched it over the made-up beds and rectified down to the centimetre any possible deviations. Rather than a cause of torment, this maniacal order seemed absurd and grotesque. In fact, the mattress levelled out with so much care had no consistency whatsoever, and in the evening, under the weight of the bodies, it immediately flattened down to the slats that supported it. As a matter of fact, one slept on wood."[1]

In another sense, isolation was absolute. Whenever the concentration camps were established close to civilian populations, care was taken to build particularly high walls. Nobody should be able to spy on what was going on inside. None of the prisoners could leave the camp unaccompanied. Anyone released was sworn to silence under threat of re-imprisonment from which there would be no return. Conversely, with the exception of a few rare visits which were painstakingly prepared and strictly vetted, no outsider was allowed to enter the camp. No judge or public prosecutor was admitted; no criminal lawyer, no journalist, no welfare worker. There could be no visits from spouses or friends. The few letters prisoners may have been able to write were subject to heavy censorship.

In every modern civilian society, the interaction between public and private life is more or less taken for granted. While the public element permits a certain degree of legal and moral control over those in power, privacy constitutes the basis of individuality. Without outside interference we are allowed to behave as we wish. By deliberately destroying both the public and the private sphere, the concentration camp created a terrible breakdown of social mores. The destruction of the private and the personal renders the individual part of a faceless mass in which numbers take the place of names. The practicalities of this transformation are described by Pastor Werner Koch, who was interned at Sachsenhausen:

"I suffered the shock of initiation on 13 February 1937 with the first blows and kicks and the realisation that my name had been virtually extinguished; from now on I was to be known only as No 392. The hair my bride had found so beautiful was shorn and my head shaved. In other words, the 'warm welcome' of the SS – shouting, beating and sadistically grinning, the ceremony of total humiliation and depersonalisation which engulfed all newcomers – had shattered my life within the space of just two hours. The last vestige of human rights had fallen to the ground with the last lock of hair. Like all the other prisoners, I was now defenceless and vulnerable to the boundless indiscriminate caprice of SS rule."[2]

His testimony exemplifies what the architecture of the concentration camp betrays: where the private and the personal have been destroyed, individuality is an aberration, to be broken, trampled underfoot, eliminated. With the loss of public control, achieved by the isolation of the camp from the outside world, order becomes arbitrary. It becomes the responsibility of those who rule with unmitigated power. These men do what they want. They are masters over life and death as long as they enjoy the protection of their superiors, right up to the level of *Reichsführer SS* Heinrich Himmler.

When the norms of civilian society – whether they take the forms of religious faith or legal jurisdiction or civil morality – stop at the walls of the concentration camp, order itself becomes arbitrary. All that remains is the order that must be obeyed. Theodor Eicke, commandant of Dachau from 1933, later inspector of all concentration camps and the SS guards, had his letter-heads printed with the words: *Es gibt nur eines, das Gültigkeit hat: der Befehl!* The only thing that counts is an order!

In the world of the concentration camp, the order, in normative terms, emerged out of nothing.[3] It was the product of pure whim. Because every SS man could give orders as he wished to any prisoner, a confusing jungle of instructions sprang up in which nobody could find their way around: a systematically ordered superstructure with chaotic consequences, in some cases life-threatening, particularly for the new arrivals so abruptly wrenched from their familiar surroundings and completely disoriented. It led to situations in which the only available choice was between violating one order or another. For example: an SS man would snatch a prisoner's cap from his head and throw it into the death zone by the fence. If the prisoner ran there to retrieve it, he would be shot. If the prisoner was seen without a cap, he would most likely be subject to a savage beating or some other draconian punishment.

A kind of sport developed among the work squads outside the camp, which were surrounded by guards. In this case, if the prisoner ran to retrieve a cap thrown beyond their lines, he was shot "attempting to escape". It was a popular pastime, especially as the prevention of an escape attempt was rewarded with leave or some other bonus. The SS men called this *Mützenjagd* (hat-hunting) or *Hasenschiessen* (hare-shooting).

It is often asked how people could possibly have behaved so barbarically, people who were by no means sadistic criminals but in fact so ordinary that after 1945 they were able to lead normal lives in civilian society without attracting any attention unless their past happened to be discovered by chance. The question is probably wrong. Maybe it should be turned around, and we should ask instead how people could arm themselves against the lure of cruelty when tempted with absolute power? How could they resist when incessantly goaded by superiors and comrades to act tough in order to belong to an elite which was, in any case, dealing not with individuals, but with numbers? "Power corrupts", as we know, "and absolute power corrupts absolutely". Who amongst us can be sure, if he has never been tried, that he would have stood the test of humanity? To stand firm against such corruption takes great strength of character.

But how could such character develop in the first place? The SS preferred to recruit young and impressionable men – volunteers aged between 16 and 19 – who, having initially been "polished" by harsh training, then found their place in a kind of *Kamaraderie der Härte* (iron comradeship) and nurtured their self-esteem by wielding power. In fact, even their leaders themselves were still very young. When the Nazis came to power in 1933, Himmler was 32, Rudolf Höss – later commandant of Auschwitz – was also 32, Reinhard Heydrich was 28 and Adolf Eichmann 26.

The isolation of the concentration camp created an arcanum; it carried with it the mystique of power. Apart from those directly involved, nobody knew exactly what was going on there. The concentration camps were black holes within civilian society. It was certainly no secret that they existed, and that opponents of the Reich were subject to "harsh treatment" there. This much knowledge was desirable as a deterrent; the mixture of knowing and not knowing allowed the camps to have their terrorising effect on the outside world. They were intended to instil fear in the enemies of the National Socialism, paralysing their actions, sealing their lips – and they succeeded in doing so. After all, everybody knew or had heard of somebody who had been "taken away" in the early hours of the morning, never to return. Everybody knew that even a joke against the Führer, or a murmur of discontent could lead to denunciation, arrest and imprisonment in that void referred to as KZ. The deterrent effect is reflected in a well-known Bavarian rhyme which went:

> *Lieber Gott, mach mich stumm,*
> *das ich nicht nach Dachau kumm.*

> *(Dear God, make me mute,*
> *so I don't get sent to Dachau)*

Not daring to speak out, over a period of years, sooner or later silenced the voice of inner resistance as well.

The pictures in this book begin in Dachau. They lead us to other concentration camps in German-occupied Europe before returning to *Mitteldeutschland.* Mittelbau-Dora and Bergen-Belsen are the last stations. In this respect, the photos themselves reflect the tide of history described below.

Dachau was the first camp in which the SS concept of *Ordnung* (order) was implemented. It became the prototype on which all the other camps were based. Their aims were the persecution and annihilation of the political opposition. Right from the start, there was never any doubt as to the nature of this objective. Soon after the Nazis came to power, Hermann Göring, Prussian minister of the interior and chief of police, declared in a public address: "People and comrades, my measures will not be weakened by any legal reservations. I am not here to practise justice, but to destroy and exterminate, and nothing else!…This is not a struggle to be waged by police measures. A bourgeois state might have done so. Certainly, I shall also make use of state and police powers – let that be clear to you Communists in case you jump to the wrong conclusions – but the struggle to the death I am about to unleash against you is one I shall wage with the rank and file: the Brownshirts."[4]

With these words, he gave free rein to violence and tyranny. What he was referring to was the mass organisation of the SA, whose gangs of thugs formed the National Socialists' private army. The SA had set up the first "unauthorised" camp. But their rivalry, with the *Wehrmacht* on the one hand and the SS on the other, weakened the power of the SA, which was finally broken by the Röhm Affair in the summer of 1934 – the first open series of murders in the Third Reich. From then on, the SS ruled triumphant. Göring appealed to the police in his decree of 17 February 1933: "Police officers who make use of firearms in the exercise of their (political rather than police) duties will be covered by me without regard for the consequence of the use of firearms; on the other hand, anyone who fails in his duty as a result of misplaced consideration can expect to face disciplinary action."

Consequently, the first concentration camp prisoners were primarily political opponents, most of them communists, social democrats and trade union leaders. The consolidation of the regime – whose restitution of "law and order" was enthusiastically welcomed by the majority of Germans – led to a climate of resignation amongst many. Rudolf Höss, then on a tour of service in Dachau, was probably not far wrong in his observation that "Once they had realised their world was shattered, all they wanted was to return to their families and be able to go about a decent job in peace and quiet. In my opinion, after 1935/36, they could quite easily have released three quarters of the political prisoners in Dachau without posing the slightest threat to the Third Reich."[5] Indeed, the number of prisoners did actually fall from around 27,000 in the summer of 1933 to 7,500 in early 1937.

Given a population totalling 66 million, this figure may sound astonishingly low. It reflects not only the sense of security that had already taken hold, but also, importantly, the successes achieved by the regime both in home affairs and foreign relations, particularly with regard to combatting unemployment and rebuilding military strength. Apart from the occasional isolated incident, generally local and due in some small degree to incompetent and corrupt officials, the vast majority of Germans were obedient to the regime – most of them out of faith in the dictatorship. Adolf Hitler's successes gave him the semblance of a farsighted politician and any irritation over local party officials could be conveniently dismissed with the words "If the *Führer* knew…" On the other hand, nobody knew the number of prisoners; the deterrent effect of the concentration camps was maintained.

Nevertheless, a change occurred in 1937 which caused the number of prisoners to swell again. New categories of prisoner were invented and interned: occupational criminals, "social deviants" (referring to vagrants and beggars as well as to people who had been denounced as "workshy"), homosexuals and Jehova's Witnesses who were conscientious objectors. As none of these groups actually posed a political threat, it may be assumed that those in power meant to increase the number of prison camp inmates as a deterrent at a time when the regime was preparing for war. Apart from which, a crackdown on criminals, the "workshy" and "social deviants" tends to be popular at any time. By October 1938, the number of prisoners had risen to 24,000. Of course, the *Anschluss* of Austria in March 1938 also played a role; the first concentration camp outside the former Reich borders was established soon afterwards at Mauthausen near Linz.

Inside the camp, the various different categories of prisoner were indicated by coloured triangles worn on the left jacket breast and sometimes on the right trouser leg as well. Red for politicals, green for criminals, black for social deviants, violet for Jehova's Witnesses, pink for homosexuals. The Jews were made to wear the yellow star. There were also additional penalty markings for violation of camp regulations and those suspected of planning to escape had a red and white target painted or sewn on front and back.

"Colours, markings, special signs – in this respect the entire concentration camp was a madhouse. Sometimes veritable rainbows were created: for example, there was a Jewish Jehovah's Witness in contravention of the Nuremberg race laws with a penalty marking and a target!"[6]

All these different categories were not only a source of absurdity, but also of deadly rivalry, particularly between the *Reds* (politicals) and the *Greens* (criminals). Dachau, Sachsenhausen and, intermittently, Buchenwald, were regarded as *Red,* while Mauthausen, Flossenbürg, Gross-Rosen and Neuengamme were predominantly *Green* camps. There were never any concentration camps intended solely for one specific category; in fact, the SS took particular care to ensure that they could exploit inter-group rivalry for their own purposes.

One further factor should be pointed out here, because it sheds some light on the system of justice – or rather injustice – which prevailed in the Third Reich. Sometimes, courts would impose punishments which, though harsh by traditional standards, unwittingly saved the lives of the accused. Conventional prisons were still places of "normal" punishment governed by the rule of law.[7] Anyone found innocent before a court of law or released from prison could still be arrested by the secret police – the *Gestapo* – at any time and sent to a concentration camp where no normal rule prevailed.

The pogroms of *Kristallnacht* on 9 November 1933 saw the first mass deportation of Jews to concentration camps – about 35,000. They were referred to as the *Aktionsjuden* or *Novemberjuden.* At this point, there was not – or not yet – any question of systematic mass murder; the aim was forced emigration and sequestration of their property. The number of camp inmates therefore fell again in the weeks and months that followed, reaching some 25,000 on 1 September 1939.

The outbreak of war brought a dramatic turn of events. First of all, the concentration camp populations became increasingly international as the German army moved further on. German inmates became a minority of between 5 and 10 per cent. From now on, Polish and, from 1941, Soviet prisoners accounted for the majority of those interned. There was also an increasing influx of prisoners from the northern, western and southern European countries.

Secondly, the overall number of prisoners increased. Having stabilised at around 60,000, the figure reached 115,000 in August 1942. The camps became permanently overfilled, leading inevitably to a deterioration in living conditions. But this was by no means the final stage. The WVHA *(Wirtschaftsverwaltungshauptamt),* the main administrative office of the SS, which had been in charge of the camps since March 1942, recorded 524,286 prisoners in August 1944 and in its last head count on 15 January 1944 put the figure at 714,211.

Thirdly, conditions of imprisonment and labour became increasingly severe, while food rations were continuously reduced. Hunger became a permanent factor. In the later phase, it was so acute that prisoners weakened and died within the space of a few weeks. Malnutrition and inadequate sanitation facilitated the spread of disease, particularly dysentery and typhus. Mortality rates reached unprecedented levels. Within the first three and a half months of 1945 prior to the liberation of Buchenwald, 13,056 of the 43,823 prisoners died. In Dachau 15,384 out of 30,958 died. Towards the end, supplies dried up completely. This happened, for example, in Bergen-Belsen, where convoys were constantly arriving from other camps. Here, between January and the liberation of the camp by British troops on 15 April 1945, some 35,000 prisoners perished and a further 14,000 died by 20 June 1945 in spite of the immediate measures taken to save them. Conservative estimates put the number of deaths at 1,100,000 out of a concentration camp population of 1,650,000. In other words, two thirds did not survive.

Admittedly, what we are talking about here is a "normal" concentration camp. From 1941 onwards, there were also extermination camps such as Kulmhof (Chełmno), Bełzec, Sobibór and Treblinka in operation, where prisoners were generally killed on arrival. In some cases, concentration camps and extermination camps existed side by side, as in Auschwitz. This dual system permitted a more "rational" approach; prisoners underwent selection on the ramp as they arrived by train and the strongest – usually the younger men and women – were sent to the labour camp. All the others were sent straight to the gas chambers. At least three million people were killed in the extermination camps alone, most of them Jews.

With the war, the work also changed. The very idea of freedom through labour had never been anything but a cynical slogan right from the start. Whether they worked on the moors or in the stone quarries, the aim was not so much one of productivity as of pushing the prisoners to the brink of exhaustion, and beyond. Work remained "unmechanised", which meant that people were forced to undertake tasks machines could do – such as pushing the rollers in road construction. The Sisyphean toil by which the norm is tranformed into its very opposite is described by Wolfgang Sofsky:

"The toil of Sisyphus is a labour of terror in its purest and most unadulterated form, void of any productive side effect. It has no other aim but that of tormenting and exhausting the prisoners. For the oppressors, it was a welcome invitation to violence, for the oppressed an endless torture which made the utter futility of their efforts blatantly obvious to them. In Dachau, prisoners were made to push a rubber-wheeled cart – the infamous Moor Express – laden with stones, back and forth through a deep mire. In other camps, the prisoners had to build stone walls and demolish them again next day only to build them again on the third day. Prisoners were forced to carry heavy railway sleepers back and forth at a running march, dig pits and fill them in again, or move piles of sand from one place to another. Sisyphean labours dismantle the fundamental structure of human work as a means to an end. Endeavour becomes effort for its own sake."[8]

By way of summary, Sofsky says: "Work is usually aimed at repairing a defect, filling a gap, overcoming a shortage. It serves a purpose beyond itself, the satisfaction of needs, delayed until the results have been achieved … work is a targeted, planned and constant activity which people experience as a burden. They accept it voluntarily or by force of circumstance in order to earn a living, in order to survive, in order to create the conditions for a better life."

In the concentration camp, it was a different matter. "The objective of work was not profit, benefit, life, but pure loss, the sovereignty that leaves all purpose behind: Death. The regime of terror was interested less in achievement than in the process of work, the exhaustion of labour. This placed the prisoners in an almost insoluble dilemma. Anyone who could no longer work was superfluous. He was selected and killed. But those who could work were exhausted within a matter of weeks unless they succeeded in being allocated to a protected *Kommando* or squad. Work did not secure life, but ruined it. Only those who avoided work could keep up the reserves of strength that work destroyed and could maintain the ability to work which protected them from death."[9]

In the course of the war, a change occurred – a change that became more marked as Germany's military situation deteriorated. Prisoners began being used as slave labour for the arms industry. The conversion of concentration camps for this purpose from March 1942 onwards was a sign of this change. Prisoners were hired out to arms manufacturers and munitions producers of all kinds. In connection with this work, more and more satellites were established for the camps. Occasionally, it was even possible to protect people from SS attacks and save them on grounds that their work was "important to the war cause". This was where people like Berthold Beitz or Oskar Schindler could act.

Nevertheless, this was very much the exception rather than the rule. The established principle of "annihiliation through labour" prevailed right to the end.

In retrospect, Rudolf Höss complained about the contradictory objectives and inconsistent orders of the *Reichsführer SS:*

"One order: increase working hours to 12 hours and severely punish any laziness. Another order: increase bonuses and create brothels to motivate efficiency. One order: prohibit procurement of additional available foods to supplement the prisoners' diet in order to ensure that the hard working civilian population is not deprived. Another order: the commandant is to ensure every effort to supplement the prisoners' official rations by procuring available foods and gathering wild vegetables. One order: given the importance of the armaments project, no consideration can be given to the health of the prisoners. Another order: in order to keep prisoners useful to the armaments project for as long as possible, overwork in industry must be curbed."[10]

This development culminated in the Mittelbau-Dora camp in the Southern Harz mountains. It was here, towards the end of the war, that labour was directed at developing Wernher von Braun's V2 rocket. Work was carried out in underground caverns to protect Germany's most important arms project against Allied bombings. The filth, starvation and lack of fresh air constituted conditions which defy description. "Between September 1943 and April 1945, within a period of little more than 18 months, at least 16,000 people were killed in the Mittelbau-Dora complex, on liquidation or evacuation transports."[11]

From the point of view of arms production, this may be regarded as grotesque mismanagement and a monstrous waste of labour resources. But was not the real war the one being waged to destroy human life?

Power and Death

The history of mankind is a tale of power and impotence, of rule and subjugation. Blood has been shed from time immemorial. We know of cruel tyrants, of conquerors and their underlings down the ages. Within our own culture alone, the Crusaders killed with the battle cry "God's will", the Inquisition turned to torture, witches were burned at the stake, Spanish *conquistadores* crushed the ancient civilisation of the Aztecs and the Incas, the North American Indians were all but wiped out, people have been enslaved and pogroms against the Jews unleashed time and time again. Terror and the guillotine have ruled in the name of liberty and civil rights.

This does not mean that the Nazi concentration camps and extermination camps were nothing new. They were new indeed. What shocks us immediately is their sheer efficiency. Their modern power. What is new is the fact that we possess the technical means – railways as mass transport systems and poison gas – to murder people under such industrial conditions. Yet there is another, more important factor. Until now, power – even the dark force of violent power – has served as a means to achieve some recognisable end within a given historical context: usurping a royal throne, conquering rich provinces, seizing wealth, imposing a religious faith, paving the way for a better society. To kill for the sake of killing alone was always regarded as a sign of sickness, madness, bestiality – and those who indulged in such acts were destroyed like rabid dogs.

Yet in Hitler's *Weltanschauung* and in the practice of the Third Reich, there is no promise of any goal beyond that of power itself, no image, however illusory, of a better society. There is nothing but the constant and unceasing Darwinian struggle for survival of the fittest in which the strong is the victor and the weak deserves no more than slavery or death. Hitler even said of his own people that they deserved just such a fate if they should fail in their struggle.

It is in this that the Nazi concentration camps differ fundamentally from the Soviet *gulags*. In terms of numbers alone, the *gulags* may have cost as many or even more lives than the German concentration camps and extermination camps. Even in the 50s, the French sociologist Jules Monnerot said: "In order to excuse warlike actions, concentration-camp practices, police torture and the re-emergence of slavery, one needs nothing less than a promise of paradise. In this way, a direct connection is created between the assurance of salvation and human cruelty."[12] No matter how appalling and inexcusable that may be, it still works on an ancient and somehow comprehensible principle aimed at industrialising the Soviet Union and creating the promised new society. To this end, losses were taken into account.

As Auschwitz survivor Primo Levi wrote: "Work was not paid; that is, it was slave work, one of the three purposes of the concentrationary system. The other two were the elimination of political adversaries and the extermination of the so-called inferior races. ... the Soviet concentrationary regime differed from the Nazi regime essentially because of the absence of the third term and the prevalence of the first."[13] It went even further than that: the aim of productively used slave labour at first played only a secondary role, if any, in the SS state. Only in future plans for the time after the *Endsieg* (final victory) was there a vision of enslaving the Eastern Europeans – Poles and Russians – in the service of the "master race". It was probably for this reason that the Emslandlager was dissolved so soon and never re-established. For there, however barbaric the conditions of labour may have been, the cultivation of moorland was actually productive. Such productive work was to be the preserve of honourable Germans, as it was in the *Reichsarbeitsdienst.* It was only the later phase of the war, when Primo Levi was interned, that led, by necessity, to slave labour for the arms industry.

If those in power acknowledge no higher instance and dismiss all aims they might serve, if power is an end in itself and becomes *absolute* in a historically new sense, then it needs a radically new form of instrumentation. Neither the German *Wehrmacht,* the state's bureaucratic machinery nor the judiciary lent themselves to such a purpose. Efficient as they might be, they originated in other, primarily Prussian, traditions which could not be dismantled easily or quickly and which therefore survived through to the end of the Third Reich.[14]

That new instrument of power, with neither tradition nor precedent, was the SS, without which the system of concentration camps it developed would have been inconceivable. As early as 1946, Eugen Kogon coined the fitting description of the "SS State" in his analysis of the concentration camp system.[15] The SS was the bedrock, the source and the very core of power in the Third Reich. It was only by a long and increasingly ambivalent process of dismantling their traditions that the other instruments of power could be included – the *Wehrmacht* following the start of the campaign against the Soviet Union in 1941.

It was in the concentration camps that the ideal of the "SS State" was developed in exemplary fashion: absolute power and total subjugation, the relationship between oppressor and oppressed, between master race and sub-human. Absolute power also involved the power over life and death. Right from the start, the freedom to kill was a characteristic of the camp, in deliberate breach of the taboo that is the fundamental principle of community: Thou shalt not kill. Consequently, the death cells, the execution blocks and the gallows were already in place long before there were gas chambers and before the mass production of Death began.

The breach of taboo had its symbolic expression in the Death Head emblem of the camp guards. In fact, since 1936, their official designation had been SS-*Totenkopfverband* (SS Death Head Unit). The photo on page 147 shows the SS officers' mess where they could be found eating and drinking convivially, singing and laughing, perhaps even telling each other of the latest jokes they had played on the prisoners. There, below the eagle with the swastika, is their motto *"Meine Ehre heisst Treue"* (My Honour is Loyalty), and the menacing Death Head.

From the freedom to kill in single isolated cases, to murder on a scale so vast that it is no longer an act, but merely an activity, is a straight path. Once the taboo has been broken, there is no stopping. It becomes irrelevant who is the victim. Systematic killing did not actually begin with the Jews, but with the mentally handicapped. The so-called "euthanasia programme" code-named *Aktion T4* began at the outbreak of war because: "the world is watching the events of war and the value of human life weighs less." In the annihilation of mental patients, methods were tested which were later to be used on a far greater scale, including murder by poison gas. Following protests from the civilian population – including the courageous sermons held by Graf Galen, Bishop of Münster – *Aktion T4* was officially ceased in August 1941. By then, 70,273 patients of mental hospitals had been killed.

It is remarkable how smoothly the transition was made. For example, when gypsies were pronounced "life without value" the Sinti and Roma were soon caught up in the machinery of death. Orders were orders and no preliminary propaganda, such as that which had been directed against the Jews, seemed necessary. The treatment of Polish and Russian prisoners of war was accepted just as unquestioningly.

By breaching the taboo of killing, a society of conspiracy and connivance was created. By making murder an objective and rational activity, a special kind of honour and even glory could be attached to it, albeit one which had to be concealed from an incomprehending world – a silence which, in turn, became exalted as a badge of honour. In a confidential speech addressed to senior SS officers, Heinrich Himmler said:

"I wish to speak to you of a very grave matter. Among ourselves, it should be mentioned quite frankly, and yet we will never speak of it publicly… I mean the evacuation of the Jews, the extermination of the Jewish race. It's one of those things it is easy to talk about. 'The Jewish race is being exterminated', says one Party member, 'that's quite clear, it's in our programme – elimination of the Jews and we're doing it, exterminating them.' And then they come, eighty million worthy Germans, and each one has his decent Jew. Of course the others are vermin, but this one is an A-1 Jew. – Not one of all those who talk this way has watched it, not one of them has gone through it. Most of you know what it means when one hundred corpses are lying side by side, or five hundred, or one thousand. To have stuck it out and at the same time – apart from exceptions caused by human weakness – to have remained *decent* fellows, that is what has made us hard. This is a *page of glory* in our history which has never been written and is never to be written."[16]

This speech unequivocally asserts the claim to have been ennobled as an elite through killing. It is consistent. Absolute power as the ideal of the SS State manifests itself in practice, in the power over life and death.

With the claim to have remained "decent", Himmler means incorruptible in the sense that killing was permitted, but personal enrichment from the victims was not. In actual practice, corruption was rife. Oskar Schindler, for example, was able to save Jewish lives by bribing SS officers. Rudolf Höss, commandant of Auschwitz, described the procedure of mass killing at some length (cited below). It should be borne in mind when reading this quotation that the victims had been told, before deportation, that they were being taken to a new and safe home, which is why they had brought with them any valuables they possessed, including money earned from the sale of the possessions they had been unable to carry.

"The valuables found, especially in the case of transports of Jews from the West, were extremely valuable – jewels worth millions, diamond-studded watches, gold and platinum watches of immeasurable value, rings, earrings, necklaces of great rarity. Currency worth millions from all different countries. Often, one person would have hundreds of thousands worth of cash, mostly in 1000 dollar bills. There was no hiding place in clothing, baggage, or the human body that was not used. (…) After sorting following a major [extermination] *Aktion,* the valuables and the money were packed in cases and sent to the WVHA [SS administrative HQ] in Berlin, and from there to the *Reichsbank.* There was a special department in the *Reichsbank* which dealt only with these things from the Jewish *Aktionen.* As I once heard from Eichmann, jewellery and currency were traded in Switzerland and controlled the entire Swiss jewellery market. The normal watches were also sent to Sachsenhausen in their thousands. There was a large clockmaking workshop there, run by hundreds of prisoners … who sorted and repaired these watches. Most of them were sent to the front for the use of the *Waffen-SS* and the army. (…) Dental gold was melted down into bars by the dentists in the SS unit and handed over once a month to the head of the medical division. Precious stones of incredible value were also found in the filled teeth (…) For the camp itself, these Jewish valuables were a source of enormous and insurmountable difficulties. It was demoralising for the SS men who were not always strong enough to resist the temptation of these readily available Jewish valuables. Even the death penalty and severest prison sentences were not an adequate deterrent. The Jewish valuables offered the prisoners tremendous opportunities. Most escapes are probably linked with this. The easily accessible money or watches, rings and so on were used to barter with SS men and civilian workers. Alcohol, tobacco, food, false papers, weapons and ammunition were commonplace. In Birkenau, the male prisoners used this as a means of getting access to the women's camp at night and they even bought the favours of some female supervisors. Of course, this adversely affected discipline in the camp. Those in possession of valuables could purchase the benevolence of the *Kapos* and the *Blockälteste* and could even buy themselves into the infirmary with the best of service. In spite of rigorous controls, this situation could not be ended. The Jews' gold became the downfall of the camp."[17]

Once again, it would seem, the Jews were to be blamed for everything, even as the victims of their own mass murder. With the logic of horror, many prisoners actually survived on the bedrock of death, for "the more the people brought with them on the death trains, the better it was for the camp. The mass death of the Jews was one of the most important elements of basic survival for the camp."[18]

Of course, the commandant of Auschwitz claims to have remained "decent". That may certainly be called into question. Even if he did not profit directly from the victims, he indisputably led a life of feudal comfort with his wife and children at the very brink of the hell on earth he was responsible for running. Sighing under the burden of his responsibilities, he said: "Yes, my family was well off in Auschwitz. All the wishes of my wife and children were fulfilled. The children could live a carefree life. My wife had her garden paradise. The prisoners made every effort to do something kind for my wife and for my children and to be attentive to them."[19]

He neglects to mention that these were people trying desperately to make themselves indispensable as slaves in the hope that this might help them to survive. There were also special workshops, such as a "leather factory" which supplied luxury goods for the commandant and his family.

"When the Höss family finally had to leave their 'Auschwitz paradise' several railway carriages were needed to carry the goods they had amassed."[20]

Everyday events are in some ways even more macabre. Johann Paul Kremer, a medic from the University of Münster with a mediocre academic career worked as a doctor in Auschwitz, where he kept a diary. In it, he noted:

"20 September, 1942. Today, Sunday afternoon from 3 to 6, listened to a concert by the prisoners' orchestra in magnificent sunshine: *Kapellmeister* was the conductor of Warsaw State Opera. 80 musicians. Roast pork for lunch, baked tench for dinner."

"23 September. Took part in the 6th and 7th *Sonderaktion tonight.*" [Selections of Jews arriving on the ramp at Auschwitz-Birkenau.] *Obergruppenführer* Pohl and company arrived at the *Waffen-SS* house in the morning. (...) Dinner at 8 p.m. with *Obergruppenführer* Pohl – a real feast. Baked pike to one's heart's content, real fresh coffee, excellent beer and sandwiches."

"30 September 1942. Took part in the 8th *Sonderaktion* tonight..."

"7 October 1942. Attended the 9th *Sonderaktion* – outsiders and *Muselweiber.*" [This was a shipment of 2012 Jews from the Dutch camp of Westerbork. *Muselmänner* was the name given to camp inmates who had given up the struggle to survive and were merely vegetating towards death. *Muselweiber* were women already on the verge of death by exhaustion when they arrived from the barbaric transport. 40 men and 58 women were registered as prisoners, all the others were gassed.]

"11 October 1942. Today, Sunday lunch of roast hare – a big juicy haunch – with dumplings and red cabbage for 1.25 RM."[21]

Kremer refers several times to the parcels of soap and food he sent home to Münster from Auschwitz.

Surviving and dying

The pictures in this book are deathly still – not only metaphorically, but literally. The living are no more.

Visitors to these former concentration camps are denied this stillness. Other visitors pass by, some whispering, some talking loudly. Tour guides shepherd their groups around, their commentaries grown weary over the years. Gangs of schoolchildren run wild, seeing the excursion as a welcome break from the classroom. Yet there is a stillness, a silence.

On a cold and drizzly March day in Sachsenhausen there is nobody to be seen. Three coachloads of passengers have set off in search of a restaurant. It is then, quite unexpectedly, that the horror begins.

What would have happened to me if I had been a prisoner here? An immediate sense of relief: but you were only seventeen when the war and the terror came to an end. *So what? Persecution and destruction spared neither youth nor age. Even children were sent to the camps.*

Primo Levi tells of a prisoner who was about my age at the time, and who was known only by his number – 018:

"*Null Achtzehn* is very young, which is a grave danger. Not only because boys support exhaustion and fasting worse than adults, but even more because a long training is needed to survive here in the struggle of each one against all, a training which young people rarely have. *Null Achtzehn* is not even particularly weak, but all avoid working with him. He is indifferent to the point of not even troubling to avoid tiredness and blows or to search for food. He carries out all the orders that he is given, and it is foreseeable that when they send him to his death he will go with the same total indifference. He has not even the rudimentary astuteness of a draught-horse, which stops pulling a little before it reaches exhaustion: he pulls or carries or pushes as long as his strength allows him, then he gives way at once, without a word of warning, without lifting his sad, opaque eyes from the ground. He made me think of the sledge-dogs in London's books, who slave until the last breath and die on the track."[22]

But what would have become of a man now well into his sixties and no longer in his physical prime? What good would it have done him to be a professor or a writer? Very little, probably. The SS were uncultivated people and little gave them more pleasure than pushing intellectuals around. That allowed them to work off their inferiority complexes and savour the triumph of their power. Better to learn some skill or trade of practical use – a cook or a plumber – in order to have any chance of survival.

One reads so much of courage and steadfastness, of comradeship and altruism, even of clandestine resistance. Could I have been one of them? Would I have been steadfast? Question upon question penetrates the deathly silence of Sachsenhausen. Questions all the more troubling because there are no answers anywhere.

Little of the heroism of the survivors, so often echoed in memorial addresses, is to be seen at first glance, especially in the desperation of the late phase when hunger, disease and selections for the gas chamber made death the rule and survival the exception. If ever there was a "struggle for existence" then it was here, as Primo Levi describes so candidly: "Preferably the worst survived, the selfish, the violent, the insensitive, the collaborators of the 'grey zones', the spies. (…) I felt innocent, yes, but enrolled among the saved and therefore in permanent search of a justification in my own eyes and those of others. The worst survived – that is, the fittest; the best all died."[23]

34

One of the psychological after-effects of the camps was the survival guilt which plagued the former prisoners (rather than the former SS officers).

Not just in the late phase, but right from the start, from the moment the first prototype camp was established in Dachau, the SS had organised a kind of self-administration system amongst the prisoners and, in doing so, had established inequality and betrayal. There were *Lagerälteste* (camp elders) and *Blockälteste* (block elders) and there were the *Kapos*. The *Kapos* were prisoners put in charge of the work squads, the kitchens, the clothing store and other facilities. It was on them that the wellbeing of the prisoners depended. The expression *Kapo* itself was actually a product of SS "humour" – an abbreviation of *Kameradschaftspolizei* or "comrades' police". The expression conveys the intention. The *Kapo* was allowed to exercise powers on behalf of the SS. He could, in isolated cases, help and protect, but more frequently he would terrorise, beat and even kill. What else could be expected when it came to consolidating privileges which could be revoked at any time?

"Nobody is more conservatively concerned about his advantage than the henchman of dictatorship. He is the born accomplice, the traitor to others. The more difficult it is to attack the centre of power, the greater is his willingness to participate in the privileges of tyranny."[24]

In order to assert himself, the *Kapo* had to prove his ability to impose order, day after day, driving his fellow prisoners ruthlessly. The result was a kind of negative selection process based on the struggle for existence.

"The support of the SS had to be bought at the price of enormous dependency. Those who served the SS gave themselves up to the arbitrary capriciousness of the SS. For the *Kapo,* there could be no return to the main body of prisoners. If he was rejected by the camp administration, his life was over. The antagonism between personnel and inmates placed him in an insoluble dilemma. Anyone who had become involved with the other side and had served as their spy or henchman had lost his right to live amongst the other prisoners. The protection of the SS brought upon him the vengeance of his comrades. The *Kapo* tried to make himself indispensable by exercising his powers excessively. He was known and feared by all. But the moment the SS took away his powers, his time was up. The threat of lynching by the prisoners drove him further into the grip of the SS. The loss of inhibition where cruelty was concerned had its roots in this. In order to protect himself, the functionary had to prove himself a loyal lackey.

In order to avoid being killed, he had to remain in power at all costs and increase the terror against those below him. But the more he terrorised the prisoners, the more he faced the threat of mob justice. All that remained for him was to conform still more to those above him, with increased zeal and violence."[25]

Let those who believe they could remain without blemish in an extreme struggle for survival which they have never experienced personally, throw the first stone. In this struggle for survival, the functionary prisoner had gained an important and possibly decisive advantage. As long as he maintained his position, he was protected and, compared to his fellow prisoners, his life was one of relative ease. Naturally, other prisoners sought his favour, upon which so much – perhaps everything – depended. They gave him what they could. And so, a kind of sub-allegiance arose, which was also revocable.

"The result of this pitiless process of natural selection could be read in the statistics of *Lager* population movements. At Auschwitz, in 1944, of the old Jewish prisoners (...), the *kleine Nummer*, low numbers less than 150,000, only a few hundred had survived; not one was an ordinary *Häftling*, vegetating in the ordinary *Kommandos*, and subsisting on the normal ration. There remained only the doctors, tailors, shoemakers, musicians, cooks, young attractive homosexuals, friends or compatriots of some authority in the camp; or they were particularly pitiless, vigorous and inhuman individuals, installed (following an investiture by the SS command, which showed itself in such choices to possess satanic knowledge of human beings) in the posts of *Kapos, Blockältester* etc.; or finally, those who, without fulfilling particular functions, had always succeeded through their astuteness and energy in successfully organizing, gaining in this way, besides material advantages and reputation, the indulgence and esteem of the powerful people in the camp. Whosoever does not know how to become an *Organisator, Kombinator, Prominent* (the savage eloquence of these words!) soon becomes a *Muselmann*. In life, a third way exists, and is in fact the rule; it does not exist in the concentration camp."[26]

Auschwitz may stand for the extreme, but in principle this applied in every camp where the masters had power over life and death.

Let us look now at the daily life of the prisoner. Some insights can be gained from the way time was perceived. It is part of the *conditio humana;* what makes a man a man is that he is able to see beyond the fetters of the here and now. We are influenced by the experiences of our lives and we make future plans for our work and our holidays, for our family and our home. We take out insurance policies against the risks of life and we keep an eye on our pension benefits. But on entering a concentration camp, everything changes. Custom and experience count for nothing. All past history is cut off. This is the violent "initiation ceremony" already mentioned. A chaos of screaming and violence, of helplessness and humiliation, engulfs the new arrival. Who does not give up his sense of time, who insists on believing in what was yesterday and what will be again tomorrow, loses not only his watch, but his very life.

What prevails from now on is uncertainty. In an instant, something completely unforeseen might happen; tomorrow is merely a rumour. The normal criminal prisoner is plagued by routine and knows how long a term he has to serve his time. Not so the concentration camp prisoner. He may be released in a week, in a month, in a year, or not at all. In order to live, he has to leave his history behind him and, above all, learn to do without the future in order to concentrate fully on the present. Everything depends on not drawing attention to oneself *now* and in the next hour in order to survive the day. What else counts when the alternative is death?

Exercising power, even in normal life, involves setting other standards of time. Children have to go to bed when adults tell them to and subordinates have to keep in line with the time schedules specified by their superiors. It is not these specifications themselves, but our ability to depend on them, that allows habits and independent planning to emerge. In the camps, the boundaries of time which are the vessel of human life were shattered like jars of clay. Logically, this devastation leads down two paths to inhumanity. One is self-assertion at any price, and any means – from theft, bribery and denunciation to killing – justifies the end. The end product and symbol of this is the *Kapo.*

The other path to inhumanity is that of resignation, indifference, of being a living corpse simply waiting for death. The end product and symbol of this is the *Muselmann.* The road to that condition is straight downhill, for, as Primo Levi puts it: "To sink is the easiest of matters; it is enough to carry out all the orders one receives, to eat only the ration, to observe the discipline of the work and the camp. Experience showed that only exceptionally could one survive more than three months in this way. All the musselmans who finished in the gas chambers have the same story, or more exactly, have no story; they followed the slope down to the bottom, like streams that run down to the sea. On their entry into the camp, through basic incapacity, or by misfortune, or through some banal incident, they are overcome before they can adapt themselves; they are beaten by time, they do not begin to learn German, to disentangle the infernal knot of laws and prohibitions until their body is already in decay, and nothing can save them from selections or from death by exhaustion. Their life is short, but their number is endless; they, the *Muselmänner*, the drowned, form the backbone of the camp, an anonymous mass, continually renewed and always identical, of non-men who march and labour in silence, the divine spark dead within them, already too empty to really suffer. One hesitates to call them living; one hesitates to call their death death, in the face of which they have no fear, as they are too tired to understand. – They crowd my memory with their faceless presences, and if I could enclose all the evil of our time in one image, I would choose this image which is familiar to me: an emaciated man, with head dropped and shoulders curved, on whose face and in whose eyes not a trace of a thought is to be seen."[27]

Just one example need be told to illustrate this: "The SS man walked slowly past and looked at the *Muselmann* coming straight towards him. We all glanced left to see what would happen. And this creature with no will of his own, unthinking, walked, shod in his wooden clogs, straight into the arms of the SS man. The SS man yelled and hit him over the head with the butt of his whip. The *Muselmann* stood where he was, hardly knowing what had happened, and when he was given a second and a third blow for failing to take off his cap, his bowels emptied (he had diarrhoea). When the SS man noticed the dark stain spreading over the *Muselmann's* wooden clogs, he was beside himself with rage. He leapt at the man, kicking him in the belly and then, as he lay in his own excrement on the ground, kicking his head and chest. The *Muselmann* did not try to defend himself. At the first kick, he doubled up. A few more kicks and he was dead."[28]

A cold and drizzly March day in Sachsenhausen, now a memorial. A former camp now void of life, deathly still, full of horror, full of questions that have no answer: what would have been *my* fate as a prisoner? Which path would I have taken?

Cain and Abel   Where do we find the origins of horror? How was it possible, in the 20th century, at the very heart of Europe, for the SS State to triumph and to construct the machinery of death that operated so smoothly?

Library shelves are full of attempts to answer these questions, and heated debates have raged over the issue of whether it was unique. To claim that it is unique is a well-meaning stance intended to prevent a false sense of security and seeking to emphasise the depth of the abyss. Yet it is also a stance which may unwittingly invite us to forget. For what is truly unique can never be repeated and is buried in the sands of history. Later generations may look back in horror, in the calm reassurance that they are not personally affected. Could it be that this theory of a unique event has made us blind to future dangers? Perhaps we could say, with appropriate caution, that what happened was so unprecedented and so inconceivable that no-one foresaw it.

One particular difficulty arises from the focus on the persecution of the Jews. Yet what other way is there of seeing it? After all, the Holocaust was undeniably the focus of the mass murders, and so it is only logical that we should examine the origins of anti-Semitism. Yet it is here that some unexpected difficulties arise. Was the hatred of the Jews so much stronger in Germany than in neighbouring countries? The historian Eberhard Jäckel, who has examined the issue in depth, has written:

"After 1945, nothing seemed more logical than to put the Nazi persecution of the Jews down to a particularly virulent anti-Semitism. Historians looked for evidence and found it. Since then, more recent comparative studies have relativised the picture somewhat. Certainly, in the depression years following the establishment of the Reich, especially between 1878 and 1887, there were anti-Semitic movements and parties. But between 1903 and 1914 they went into decline and had all but disappeared by the eve of the first world war. The principle of equality before the law for Jews had never been seriously jeopardised, in spite of social discrimination. Germany did not have Russia's pogroms or France's Dreyfuss affair and even in Austria, anti-Semitism seemed stronger than in Germany. – In 1975, the American historian George L. Mosse tried to elucidate the situation by suggesting that, had people been told in 1914 that most of the European Jews were to be murdered within a generation, they would probably have retorted that the French are capable of anything. They might have suspected the Russians, the Poles or the Austrians. But the last place they would have thought of would have been Germany."[29]

This situation proved to be a trap within a trap. In Germany, the Jewish community had become more fully assimilated than elsewhere. They identified with Germany and saw themselves as patriots. It was this that made many of them refuse to believe what was happening in their own country – and they consequently failed to emigrate in time to save themselves from destruction.[30]

The difficulties continue when we consider the system of concentration camps which was developed after the Nazis came to power. The system arose as a means of countering active political opposition prior to 1933 – particularly communists and socialists, including Jews, of course, albeit as a minority. When, in November 1938, Jews began being sent to the concentration camps in large numbers for no other reason than the fact that they were Jewish, the original intention was still that of forced emigration, not murder. And so on: Auschwitz was built to crush the Polish ruling class; the destruction of the Jews followed. In other words, the concentration camps and the SS state arose independently of the persecution of the Jews; had the military campaign against the Soviet Union been successful and more prolonged, the extermination camps would probably have continued to operate after the Holocaust as well, by going on to concentrate on the "Slavonic subhumans", a trend which had in fact, already begun.

Where should we begin? In the search for the unknown perpetrator of a crime, the experienced detective applies a tried and tested golden rule: he seeks the motive. *Cui bono?* Greed and the desire to seize the victims' property certainly played a role, as it had always done in pogroms. But what happened in the Third Reich went far beyond that. The Holocaust cannot be traced back to a motive of this kind; it affected mainly the poor as well as those who had been wealthy, and any personal enrichment in the course of the murder campaigns was officially disapproved by the SS, though it was common practice.[31] On closer examination, another factor, more monstrous still, begins to take shape unequivocally: the sense of power or self-esteem based on wielding power over life and death.

It is part of the human condition that, in order to get through life, one has to build up a sense of self-esteem. This is done in a positive sense through the affection and trust of others, through achievement and success. But if it fails, it can become negative: one imagines enemies conspiring together with uncanny powers to prevent all success and recognition. Fighting them becomes a way of regaining the lost meaning of life: the enemy gives the individual and the mass a sense of identity. Triumph is achieved by gaining power over enemies; one's own significance is reflected in the very fear that is an echo of power[32] and the greatest, most absolute and consummate triumph – the *final solution* of such power – consists in killing the enemy.

Power thus becomes a mainstay of self-esteem. We should bear in mind that the central event in the history of National Socialism was celebrated as a *seizure of power.* For it was this alone, seizing and asserting power, that counted. Correspondingly, the system of the concentration camps was evidence of absolute power and was as necessary to German domestic policy as the war of aggression was to foreign policy.

While we may talk of an injured, mad or perverted sense of self-esteem, there can nevertheless be no doubt that it is a human possibility. Even the uncanny tale of the original crime of aggression relates it:

"And in process of time it came to pass, that Cain brought of the fruit of the ground and offering unto the Lord.

And Abel, he also brought of the firstlings of his flock and of the fat thereof. And the Lord had respect unto Abel and to his offering:

But unto Cain and his offering he had not respect. And Cain was very wroth, and his countenance fell.

And the Lord said unto Cain, Why art thou wroth? and why is thy countenance fallen?

If thou doest well, shalt thou not be accepted? and if thou doest not well, sin lieth at the door. And unto thee shall be his desire, and thou shalt rule over him.

And Cain talked with Abel his brother: and it came to pass, when they were in the field, that Cain rose up against Abel his brother, and slew him."

It is a heinous tale – a tale of self-esteem destroyed and catastrophe unleashed against a brother who has become the object of envy and hate. He becomes both enemy and scapegoat and, at the same time, an *ersatz* sense of self-esteem is sought in the power to kill him.

However, if it is a human possibility, then the question arises as to why it should have happened in Germany. Is it due to some natural characteristic of the Germans? Hardly. In his novel *L'auberge rouge,* Balzac introduces the narrator – portly Mr Hermann, a merchant from Nuremberg – as "a true son of noble and pure Germania, which is so full of honourable characters, whose peace-loving customs cannot be denied even after seven invasions." It was a common and widespread view of the Germans at one time. Why the change? What happened? How did portly Mr Hermann and Nuremberg become names which conjure up quite different associations in the 20th century than they did in the 19th? *Blitzkrieg* and *Endlösung* have become as firmly associated with Germany as *Bildung* and *Gemütlichkeit* once were.

Any attempt to seek an answer would require far more time and space,[33] so I shall merely outline the main points briefly here. One crucial factor was that, in the era of the nation state, Germany's history of freedom took the form of a sequence of defeats. The 1848 revolution calling for national unity and a free constitution failed. Bismarck's unification of Germany, by contrast, brought with it the triumph of an efficient and militarily powerful authoritarian state, fatefully consolidating its lasting and widespread acceptance. The Weimar Republic failed, as did the attempt on 20 July 1944 to assassinate Hitler and overthrow the regime of violence from within. After 1945, democracy and socialism were introduced at the point of a bayonet by the Allied victors and West Germany chose yet another day of failure – the quashed East German revolt of 17 June 1953 – as a national holiday. Something new happened in the autumn of 1989: citizens rose up and showed civil courage, bringing down a perfectly organised authoritarian state and banishing its self-appointed leaders. In this way, perhaps, the second German nation state may face a better future than the first.[34]

By way of comparison, almost everywhere, the self-awareness and self-esteem of western nations is based on the memory of some origin of uprising – a founding myth, as it were, of freedom fought for and won: the Swiss sagas of Tell and Winkelried, the Dutch struggle for independence against Habsburg Spain, England's Glorious Revolution, the French Revolution, the American War of Independence.

Each young person, each new generation first has to gain independence; they must stand on their own two feet and become responsible from within rather than just on outward appearances. The same is true of nations. In order to become politically adult and mature as a nation, it would seem that they have to behead a king or dethrone a tyrant, impose obedience to God or the populace on the ruling class and cast off foreign rule. Only when they have done so can they gain their own identity and create a stable sense of self-esteem.

The matter becomes even clearer if one examines the interaction between a sense of power and the projected image of the enemy. The glory of military power in Bismarck's unification was the triumph over the "arch enemy" France at the decisive Battle of Sedan, symbolised from then on by the celebration of "Sedan Day" – in fact the only national holiday ever to have won any real popularity in Germany. At the turn of the century, theologist and philosopher Ernst Troeltsch examined what he regarded as Bismarck's fundamental political re-education of Germany with a critical eye:

"Its point was precisely that the essence of the state is power, that its very backbone is an efficient army, that it can counter threats from outside and inside only by calculated and ruthless measures… It is an ideal subordinating everything, with neither prejudice nor bias, to the sole political maxim of power which is both permanent and superior to every opponent." In this respect, the obsession with power for its own sake "has become accepted even by us as we pepper our theories with Nietzschean superman morality or Darwinistic survival of the fittest and tend to identify all too easily with those ideals of laconic determination and bureaucratic power which the coming generation of the ruling classes possesses in ample degree."[35]

In the Wilhelmine period following the fall of Bismarck, a new enemy began to be projected – England. The empire that ruled the waves stood in the way of Germany's nascent dreams of becoming a world power. It was against England that Wilhelmine Germany directed its grandest power project, the construction of a battle fleet, and when the first world war broke out, a vitriolic hatred of England exploded under the motto *Perfides Albion! Gott strafe England!* (Perfidious Albion! God punish England!)

The war proved the project to be no more than a castle in the air and the instrument of power to be impotent; the fleet languished in the ports and eventually became the hotbed of revolution. The Germans keenly felt that defeat in a war so bravely fought was undeserved and they regarded the collapse of imperial power and the proclamation of the Republic on 9 November 1918 as nothing short of a monstrous injustice. Unable to project the image of an unequivocal enemy, the new democratic constitutional state came to epitomise the enemy itself and was denounced as "un-German" and despicable. Anyone who had been even remotely involved in the 1918 coup or who was regarded to have profited from it, was declared a *Novemberverbrecher* (November criminal) and was subject, in word, if not in deed, to vehmic justice.

Hitler, a man deft at recognising the value of symbols and their emotive power, deliberately engineered his Munich *Bierkeller* putsch of 1923 to fall on a date of considerable emotional importance to the German people, thereby projecting himself as the redeemer of 9 November. Later, after he took power, the events of 1923 – the *Marsch auf die Feldherrnhalle* – were pompously re-enacted every year like a passion play of death and resurrection. On the 20th anniversary of the putsch, the *Kristallnacht* of 1938, the houses of God – the synagogues – were burned as a sign of victory by the German counterrevolution that now sought to avenge a purported crime by committing a real one. All in all, the destruction of the Weimar Republic and the National Socialist seizure of power can only be properly understood against the background of a national self-esteem so dependent on power that it was therefore deeply wounded by the defeat and fall of 1918.[36]

Hitler proved to be a master in the art of projecting the image of the enemy and, as such, succeeded in establishing himself as the celebrated *Führer* – the leader who would liberate the German people from their impotence. He described his tactics with cynical candour: "The art of all truly great leaders has, at all times, consisted first and foremost in their ability not to divide the attention of the people, but to concentrate it on one single enemy. The more united this use of a people's will to fight, the greater the magnetic attraction of a movement will be and the greater its force. It is part of the genius of a great leader to make even widely different enemies appear to belong to a single category, because, for those who are of weak and uncertain character, the awareness of different enemies all too easily sows doubts about their own rights. – As soon as the hesitant masses see themselves fighting against too many enemies, objectivity comes into play and they begin asking whether all the others really are in the wrong and whether their own people or their own movement really are the only ones in the right. – This is where the paralysis of their own power begins. It is for this reason that a number of inherently different enemies always have to be lumped together so that, in the eyes of the masses, the struggle is fought against one single enemy. This strengthens faith in one's own rights and increases the bitterness against the attacker of those rights."[37]

This basic principle led to such ludicrous neologisms as *jüdisch-plu-tokratisch-bolschewistisch.* Indeed, the Jews suited this purpose for a number of reasons. First of all, ancient prejudices could be revived and invoked against them and made to seem like a struggle between the forces of darkness and light. At the very least, it could be expected – correctly, as it transpired – that the persecution of the Jews would meet with little opposition. Secondly, the impression could be created that this sole enemy of old was the force behind all enemies, in east and west, in capitalism as in communism: was not the banker Rothschild a Jew, just as the grandfather of Communism, Karl Marx, had been? Thirdly, by claiming uncanny powers for the Jews, their destruction could be stylised into a heroic struggle between worlds –

even though people knew full well that the Jews were in fact a defenceless minority.

Hitler repeatedly stated that "9 November 1918 should never be repeated in German history." This meant that any power which was not to be subjugated again, but which was to assert itself in the struggle for existence, must liberate itself from all considerations of faith, morality and justice and become absolute.

The concentration camps and extermination camps were a central element in this. When the first shadow of impending defeat began to darken the triumph of conquest, Germany clung all the more desperately to the power manifested in the freedom to kill. On 20 January 1942, only a few weeks after the Germans were defeated before Moscow, on the eve of America entering the war, the Wannsee Conference was held at which the *Final Solution to the Jewish Problem* was discussed.

Epilogue   The memorials which stand where once there were concentration camps are deathly still. To hear the silence is to face the last insistent question – can history repeat itself?

It can. Barbarity is part of human nature. Here, in these places, it proved its ability to surface and become reality, given fertile soil.

Let me not be misconstrued. Let me stress once more that to deny the unique nature of the Holocaust is by no means a question of playing down or trivialising it. On the contrary, it means being constantly on the alert. In the words of Wofgang Sofsky: "A murderer who seeks to justify his action by the fact that there are other murderers does not diminish his responsibility."[38]

What we owe the victims is neither the kind of sanctimoniousness that distorts their lives and their suffering, nor any belated sense of empathy which can no longer touch them. Nor is it the transfiguration of a death which served only the perpetrators.

Above all, we should not talk of the inexplicable as though it were some mystery worked by god or the devil. What we owe the victims is an effort to understand and a watchful eye. For barbarity, whenever it returns, will do so incognito. It will seek unexpected places and disguises in order to seem honourable. What matters most is to realise in time what is happening. That applies in a double sense.

On the one hand, it is important not to remain indifferent while it is not us but others who are affected. As Pastor Martin Niemöller, who was imprisoned in Sachsenhausen and Dachau from 1937 to 1945, said in retrospect: "When the Nazis came to take away the Communists, I did not speak out, for I was not a Communist. When they came to take away the Social Democrats, I did not speak out, for I was not a Social Democrat. When they came to take away the Catholics, I did not speak out, for I was not a Catholic. When they came to take me away, there was nobody left to protest."[39]

On the other hand, resistance must be exercised before a "seizure of power". Experience has shown that, later, there is little chance because organised enthusiasm and terror stifle any rebellion. One of the righteous gentiles, Albrecht Haushofer, who paid for his resistance with his life, wrote a sonnet entitled *"Schuld"* ("Guilt") as he awaited execution:

Ich trage leicht an dem, was das Gericht
mir Schuld benennen wird: an Plan und Sorgen.
Verbrecher wäre ich, hätt ich für das Morgen
des Volkes nicht geplant aus eigner Pflicht.

Doch schuldig bin ich anders als ihr denkt,
ich mußte früher meine Pflicht erkennen,
ich mußte schärfer Unheil Unheil nennen –
mein Urteil hab ich viel zu lang gelenkt…

Ich klage mich in meinem Herzen an:
ich habe mein Gewissen lang betrogen,
ich habe mich selbst und anderen belogen –

ich kannte früh des Jammmers ganze Bahn –
ich hab gewarnt – nicht hart genug und klar!
Und heute weiß ich, was ich schuldig war…[40]

The burden of my guilt before the law
weighs light upon my shoulders: to plot
and to conspire was my duty to the people;
I would have been a criminal had I not.

I am guilty, though not the way you think,
I should have done my duty sooner, I was wrong,
I should have called the evil more clearly by its name
I hesitated to condemn for far too long.

I now accuse myself within my heart:
I have betrayed my conscience far too long
I have deceived myself and fellow man –

I knew the course of evil from the start –
My warning was not loud or clear enough!
Today I know what I was guilty of…

129

Breendonk

163

214

229

Sobibór

233

Hamburg

Fleet and
St. Michaeliskirche

Bergen-Belsen

277

London

Hamburg

Neuengamme

Westerbork

Emslandlager

Bergen-Belsen

Amsterdam

Herzogenbusch

Breendonk

Brüssel

Mittelbau-Dora

Buchenwald

Frankfurt

Paris

Flossenbürg

Nürnberg

Straßburg

Natzweiler

Dachau

München

Bern

Mailand

Kopenhagen

Danzig ● Stutthof

Ravensbrück

Sachsenhausen

Berlin

Treblinka

Warschau

Kulmhof

Sobibór

Breslau

Lubin-Maidanek

Groß-Rosen

Belzec

Theresienstadt

Prag

Krakau

Auschwitz

Linz

Mauthausen

Wien

Bratislava

Budapest

Dachau

The First Nazi concentration camp went into operation on 22 March 1933 on the outskirts of the Upper Bavarian town of Dachau. Built on the premises of a former powder and munitions factory, it had an initial capacity of 5,000 prisoners (1943: approx. 17,000). Intended for political prisoners, the camp soon included all groups branded by the regime: political opponents, Jehova's Witnesses (conscientious objectors), Jews, gypsies, handicapped, homosexuals, criminals. Reciprocal discrimination and denunciation were encouraged and group formation was difficult.

During the war, the nationalities of the "new arrivals" reflected the regime's latest military successes. The concentration camp developed into a broad network of 125 satellite camps and sub-camps supplying the South German arms industry with labour; surrounded by SS housing estates, the camp was secluded and yet, in spite of its isolated situation, it was close to the metropolitan infrastructure of nearby Munich.

The system of regulations and punishments current in Dachau was adopted by other concentration camps, as was the structure of the complex.

Being a prototype camp, Dachau also served as a training ground: trainee camp commandants were sent here for special instruction and the SS Death Head Units originated here.

Dachau was not originally planned as an extermination camp, but prisoners were "shot attempting to escape" or died of hunger, disease and exhaustion ("annihilation through work"), under torture and as victims of pseudo-scientific "research" such as decompression and refrigeration experiments.

With the decision to implement the "final solution", a crematorium and gas-chambers were built in 1942, though there is no evidence of them having been put to use. In the period up to November 1944, however, 3,225 disabled or mentally handicapped prisoners are known to have been taken to the "euthanasia institute" at Schloss Hartheim (near Linz) and gassed there. On the day Dachau was liberated (29 April 1945) the Americans found 30,000 survivors in the barracks. Up to this point in time, 206,000 registered prisoners had passed through the camp. 31,951 deaths were recorded.

Emslandlager　　Between 1933 and 1944, the Nazis built a total of 15 camps along the Ems near the Dutch border between Papenburg in the North and Lingen in the South. The camps fulfilled a number of different functions. They were concentration camps until 1934/36, prison camps until 1939, military prisons and prisoner of war camps until 1945.

In the camps of Versen and Dalum, satellites of the Neuengamme concentration camp were established in 1944/45. The concentration camps established in the summer of 1933 in Emsland by the Prussian state held primarily political prisoners (mainly from the Rhineland and the Ruhr), social democrats, communists, trade unionists, Jehova's Witnesses and others.

In 1934, the camp was converted from a concentration camp to a so-called criminals' camp, where political opponents of the Nazi regime, ethnic and religious minorities, homosexuals, "work shy" and other groups termed by the Nazis as *Volksschädlinge* (human vermin) were imprisoned.

Esterwegen remained a concentration camp until 1936, when the prisoners were transferred to Sachsenhausen to build the concentration camp there.

The nine southern camps served as PoW camps after 1939. The camps served not only the political aims of the regime, but also its economic aims. In Emsland, the prisoners, equipped only with hoes and spades, cultivated the vast moorlands. For these prisoners, the hard physical labour often meant "annihilation through work".

In the concentration and prison camps of Emsland, at least 2,387 prisoners died and in the PoW camps between 15,000 and 17,000 died.

Camp I	Börgermoor
Camp II	Aschendorfermoor
Camp III	Brual-Rhede
Camp IV	Walchum
Camp V	Neusustrum
Camp VI	Oberlangen
Camp VII	Esterwegen
Camp VIII	Wesuwe
Camp IX	Versen
Camp X	Fullen
Camp XI	Gross-Hesepe
Camp XII	Dalum
Camp XIII	Wietmarschen
Camp XIV	Bathorn
Camp XV	Alexisdorf

Sachsenhausen　　The concentration camp of Sachsenhausen was established in August/September 1936 approximately 25 kilometres north-east of Berlin and was built by prisoners of the Esterwegen-Emsland camp. Sachsenhausen was surrounded by a 2.50m high wall with electric barbed wire fencing and eight watchtowers. Originally intended to hold between 8,000 and 10,000 prisoners, some 35,000 were interned in Sachsenhausen towards the end of the war. By mid-February 1945, more than 135,000 prisoners had passed through the camp.

In its early days, Sachsenhausen held mainly political prisoners, but later included Jews, gypsies, "social deviants", criminals, Jehova's Witnesses, homosexuals, soldiers dismissed from the *Wehrmacht* and former SS men, Soviet prisoners of war and prisoners from occupied territories (Czechs, Poles, Dutch, Belgians, French, Norwegians). The inmates of the camp worked mainly in the DAW German armaments and munitions factories *(Deutsche Ausrüstungswerke)* and in a clothing factory or shoe factory. A particularly severe punishment was recruitment to the so-called *Schuhläufer-Kommando* or "boot-runner squad" in which prisoners had to test *Wehrmacht* boots on long marches. Of Sachsenhausen's 61 satellites, the main ones were the Heinkel aviation industry in Germendorf, the brickworks in Oranienburg and the DEMAG works in Falkensee.

Within the camp itself, there was a special camp for "prominent" prisoners and their families. Conditions in Sachsenhausen were catastrophic. Many prisoners died of hunger, cold, exhaustion, lack of medical treatment, were shot, hanged or tortured to death by SS member or *Funktionshäftlinge*. Prisoners who where ill or unable to work were regularly selected and killed at the camp by poison injections or in the gas-chambers built in 1943. On 6 June 1941, the *Wehrmacht* supreme command had ordered that all Soviet prisoners of war should be killed (this order was known as the *Kommissarbefehl*). In the autumn of that same year, more than 11,000 Soviet PoWs were killed by shooting them in the back of the neck in the execution block *(Genickschussanlage)* camouflaged as a medical station under the pretext of being given a "medical examination". In the period that followed, the execution block was also used to shoot prisoners who had been brought to Sachsenhausen at the orders of the RSHA *(Reichssicherheitsamt;* the head office of the Gestapo and SS) for what the Nazis referred to euphemistically as "special treatment".

As in all the major concentration camps, medical experiments were carried out on the prisoners in Sachsenhausen. The experiments included inflicting non-fatal wounds which were then deliberately contaminated to provoke gangrene, for which a new antiseptic was being developed. Many died. In the summer of 1944, four out of eight prisoners died in the course of unknown experiments. In September 1944, prisoners were wounded with poisoned munitions to determine how long the poison needed to take effect. Soviet prisoners of war were killed in tests to build a new mobile gas-chamber in the autumn of 1941. In early 1945, as the Soviet front began to close in, the SS killed a number of hospitalised inmates who were unable to walk. Those who were less seriously ill were evacuated in freight cars to other camps within the Reich (Bergen-Belsen, Dachau and Mauthausen). About 3,000 prisoners, most of them ill, were left in Sachsenhausen and were liberated by Soviet troops on 22/23 April 1945. The Nazis had evacuated most of the prisoners on foot in April 1945. Those who could not keep pace were shot at the roadside by the SS. This evacuation death-march ended in Schwerin, where the exhausted prisoners were liberated by American troops.

Buchenwald   In the summer of 1937, the concentration camp of Buchenwald was established in a forest of the Etterberg region near Weimar. In November 1939 the camp held some 12,600 prisoners, 2,400 of them Jews. Shortly before the end of the war, up to 47,000 prisoners were held in Buchenwald, many of whom were transported to other camps as Allied troops drew near. On liberation, the Americans found 21,000 survivors. The prisoners had been enslaved to the German armaments industry (DAW), or had laboured in artisanal workshops (locksmith, carpentry and others), in the extensive market garden of the camp, in livestock stalls of various kinds (including stables) and in a nearby stone quarry. The camp had about 130 satellites, some of which were at a considerable distance from the main camp.

Conditions in Buchenwald were appalling. Many prisoners died of hunger, illness (dysentry epidemics), exhaustion, maltreatment, hanging, torture, (which included being tied to trees or posts with their arms twisted behind their backs), had been shot allegedly attempting to escape, or had been killed in medical experiments. From 1941 onwards, several thousand Russian prisoners of war were shot in the back of the neck in the execution block or *Genickschussanlage* by order of the RSHA. Shootings were also carried out in the crematorium. Many prisoners were killed by injections of phenol (carbolic acid) or other poisons. Objects such as lampshades and cigarette cases were made for SS members out of tattooed human skin.

| Neuengamme | The concentration camp of Neuengamme, some 30 kilometres east of Hamburg, was a satellite of the Sachsenhausen concentration camp. Neuengamme initially held 500 prisoners, who built the camp. 87,000 male prisoners and 13,500 female prisoners from all over Europe passed through the camp. In June 1940, Neuengamme became an independent concentration camp. The prisoners produced bricks, were put to work in channelling the river Elbe and in building further satellites and camps – 74 in all – for the arms industry. |

The conditions of work, accommodation and hygiene cost many lives, as did maltreatment and murders by the SS supervisors. Many Soviet prisoners of war or political prisoners were brought to the camp by the Gestapo and were shot or hanged there. In April 1945, at the satellite set up in the school of Bullenhuserdamm in Hamburg, 20 Jewish children aged under 12 were hanged to cover up the tuberculosis experiments carried out on them. The Nazis evacuated the camp in April 1945. Most of the prisoners were loaded onto the ships *Deutschland, Cap Arcona* and *Thielbek* lying at anchor in the bay, which were hit by a British bombing raid on 3 May 1945, claiming the lives of more than 7,000 prisoners from Neuengamme. 56,000 people died in the concentration camp of Neuengamme.

| Flossenbürg | In May 1938, the concentration camp of Flossenbürg was established near Weiden (Upper Palatinate) in the immediate vicinity of a stone quarry on a mountain slope. Holding an average of between 5,000 and 6,000 prisoners, the numbers swelled in the last months of the war to between 15,000 and 18,000. In the course of time, the number of satellite work squads and sub-camps increased to more than 90. The prisoners were enslaved mainly in the arms and munitions industry, the aviation industry and oil production. The prisoners at Flossenbürg came from a number of different countries, mostly in Eastern Europe (Poles, Russians and others). In the early years, German political prisoners and, later, criminals were interned in Flossenbürg. The prisoners were put to work in the stone quarry 200 m from the camp and on various building projects. Those who fell ill or became unable to work were "selected". Often, prisoners were forced to carry out a "punishment exercise", laden with heavy stones, in a marshy hole at the bottom of the quarry, in knee-deep mud. Apart from executions, exhaustion and illness claimed a high death toll amongst the prisoners. |

On 20 April 1945, the camp was evacuated and the prisoners were transferred to Dachau on an eight-day death march. Anyone unable to keep pace was shot at the roadside. On 23 April 1945, American troops liberated the prisoners who had been left behind in the camp.

| Ravensbrück | Ravensbrück was established to the north of Fürstenberg an der Havel on 15 May 1939 as a camp for female prisoners. By the end of 1939, some 2,000 women were incarcerated at Ravensbrück. By the end of 1942, they numbered 10,800, and in 1944 some 70,000 prisoners entered the camp. According to the files of the International Red Cross, 107,753 women passed through the camp and its 42 satellites. The women came from all over Europe and were held as political prisoners, Jews, gypsies, Jehovah's Witnesses, prostitutes, criminals and other categories. They were put to work in the SS test station for food and nutrition, in the private agricultural sector and in nearby industries and firms. A small camp for male prisoners was added in March/April 1941. The women's camp was guarded mainly by SS women under supervision of a male commandant. |

Inadequate accommodation and nutrition, lack of hygiene and sanitary facilities were the main causes of the high mortality rate amongst prisoners in Ravensbrück. Punishments, torture and heavy physical work did the rest. Many died as a result of medical experiments (gangrene and wound infection experiments, sterilisation experiments on gypsies and others). Other victims were "prisoners unfit for work" and "mentally defective" prisoners who were "selected" from 1942 onwards by medical committees, allegedly for transfer to sanatoriums, but who were actually transferred to "euthanasia stations" where they were gassed. In the spring of 1945, a gas chamber was built near the crematorium. Between 2,300 and 2,400 prisoners were gassed there.

In March 1945, French and Swedish women prisoners were freed by the intervention of the Swedish Red Cross. In April 1945, as the Red Army advanced, the Nazis drove the remaining prisoners westwards on foot, but were overtaken by Soviet troops. Those prisoners who had been left behind as ill or unable to walk were liberated by the Red Army on 29/30 April.

Mauthausen

Mauthausen concentration camp was established in August 1938 some 20 km east of Linz. At the outbreak of war, Mauthausen held about 1,500 prisoners. By April 1942 5,500 prisoners were interned there. Towards the end of the war, almost 50,000 prisoners were held in cramped conditions in the main camp alone. In the largest satellite camps of Mauthausen, Gusen I and II, with a total of 56 external work squads and sub-camps, a further 24,000 prisoners were held in March 1945. They came from all over Europe (including criminal and political German prisoners, Danish police, Dutch and Hungarian Jews, Soviet prisoners of war). From July 1943 Jewish women and children were interned and transports of Soviet, Polish, Yugoslavian, Italian and French children and youths as well as Jewish-Polish gypsy children (including infants) arrived from Ravensbrück. According to the last official statistics, dated 31 March 1945, the camp held more than 1,500 children and young persons aged under 20 and more than 2,200 women.

In 1938/39, most of the prisoners were put to work on building the camp. Later, they worked in the granite quarries of the SS stoneworks (DEST) and, from around autumn 1943, they were enslaved in the arms industry (Messerschmitt AG). Nutrition was entirely inadequate, accommodation and sanitary conditions appalling. Many died of hunger and exhaustion. SS members or *Kapos* shot, hanged or beat prisoners to death in the *Wiener Graben* stone quarry. Those who were ill or unfit to work were selected and killed in "euthanasia" stations, sent to the gas chambers of the camp, killed in the mobile gas chamber operating between Mauthausen and the Gusen satellite camp (about 5 km away) or injected with poison at the camp. The execution block or *Genickschussssanlage* near the crematorium was used to shoot prisoners in the back of the neck after telling them they were being taken for medical examination. Human experiments claimed further victims.

It is no longer possible to determine exactly how many people were murdered in Mauthausen and its satellites. The official camp documents record about 71,000 deaths (the number of unregistered deaths is not known).

American soldiers arrived in Mauthausen on 7 May 1945.

Natzweiler (Struthof)

The concentration camp of Natzweiler – officially opened on 1 May 1941 – was situated near the Alsatian village of the same name in the Vosges mountains, about 50 km south-west of Strasbourg. Originally planned for the internment of 1,500 prisoners (in the autumn of 1944, it held about 7,000 prisoners, and, including the satellite camps, between 20,000 and 25,000). Prisoners of various nationalities laboured in the SS earth and stone quarries (DEST), building roads and tunnels (including caverns for the subterranean armaments industry) and in the slate quarries of the Swabian Jura. The camp had 49 satellites. Many prisoners died of hunger, illness, exhaustion, maltreatment and many were shot purportedly "attempting to escape", hung or otherwise killed.

Others were victims of medical experiments carried out on the prisoners in collaboration with the medical staff of the *Reichsuniversität* of Strasbourg: experiments were conducted with chemical weapons and a collection of skulls and skeletons was built up for "race studies". Prisoners were transferred from Auschwitz to Natzweiler expressly for this purpose and gassed in a small gas chamber with cyanide salts; the corpses were then transferred to Strasbourg for de-boning. Other experiments conducted on prisoners included typhus and yellow fever "research" and testing of phosgene gas (chlorocarbonic acid).

In September 1944, as the Allied forces drew closer, the main camp was disbanded and the prisoners transferred to the satellites. The number of victims is unknown and estimates range from between 5,000 and 6,000 to as many as 12,000.

Breendonck

In September 1940, the concentration camp of Breendonck was established about 20 km south of Antwerp on route A 12 halfway to Brussels. It had originally been built as a fort between 1906 and 1914. A large moat had been dug out around the fort and flooded, and the earth excavated was used to cover the ramparts.

While it was being used as a concentration camp, this earth (about 250,000 to 300,000 cubic metres) was removed by the prisoners. Breendonck held prisoners of various nationalities, mainly Belgians.

The first large-scale deportations from Breendonck took place in September 1941 when prisoners were transferred to the concentration camp of Neuengamme near Hamburg. Accommodation was appalling in the dark and damp casemates. There were special torture chambers where prisoners were subjected to tortures which defy description. Some 200 prisoners were shot or hanged at the camp.

The fort was evacuated on 6th May 1944 and on 31st August 1944, the first Allied troops reached Breendonck. According to Belgian estimations, Breendonck held approximately 4,000 prisoners throughout the period of its use as a concentration camp.

Herzogenbusch
('s-Hertogenbosch or Vught)

The concentration camp was opened on 5 January 1943. The first inmates were German criminal prisoners (known by the abbreviation BV = *Berufsverbrecher*) who were used as *Kapos* and *Funktionshäftlinge*. In January 1943, the first transportation of Dutch prisoners arrived in Herzogenbusch. In May 1943, Dutch women prisoners arrived, and were held at the separate women's concentration camp of Vught. In January 1943, a shipment of Jews arrived from Amsterdam. These were so called *Ziviljuden* (civilian Jews) who were held in the *Judendurchgangslager* or JDL (transit camp for Jews). From the JDL, a number of transports were made to Poland. These included a transport of Jewish children in May 1943, almost all of whom were taken to the extermination camp of Sobibór together with their parents (a total of about 3,000 persons). Further transportations of Jews to Auschwitz followed in November 1943 and in June 1944 (last transport).

The *Studentenlager* (student camps) of Herzogenbusch held mainly oppositional students and the *politische Durchgangslager* (political transit camp) was established in August 1943 for political prisoners from Dutch prisons. The *Geisellager* (hostage camp) was for persons who had been arrested as hostages in retribution for acts of sabotage or as relatives of wanted prisoners (mostly women and children). A total of about 29,500 prisoners of various categories were held at Herzogenbusch.

Many of the prisoners were sent to work for the Philips electrical company and the Escotex textile company. Conditions in the different departments of the camp varied considerably, but were generally poor. Several hundred people were executed or beaten to death in Herzogenbusch. As the Allied troops drew closer in the South of Holland in September 1944, the prisoners were evacuated by train. Most of the men were sent to Sachsenhausen and the women to Ravensbrück.

Westerbork

Westerbork was a police internment camp and a police transit camp for Jews in Drenther Heide (Netherlands). It was established in the spring of 1939 for Jewish refugees who had fled from German Reich territory since the end of 1938. From 18 May 1940 to 30 June 1942, Westerbork was the responsibility of the Dutch Ministry of Justice under German command. From 1 July 1942, the camp was taken over by the chief of security police in The Hague. Around New Year 1941/42, there were some 1,600 Jewish men, women and children in Westerbork; by the end of 1942, further barracks had been built with a capacity of at least 10,000, in which Jews of various nationalities and gypsies were interned.

The prisoners worked in the camp administration, as craftsmen and labourers in various workshops and in agriculture, gardening and road construction. Compared to other camps, conditions at Westerbork were relatively good. The camp staff comprised about ten SS members, some of them severely war-injured. They were initially assisted by Dutch personnel, whose duties were later taken over by Jewish prisoners. Dutch police officers were used to guard the outside of the camp.

On 15 July 1942, the deportation of Westerbork prisoners began by train to the extermination camps in the East, particularly Sobibór and Auschwitz. A total of 69,000 Jewish men, women and children were deported, 68,000 of whom probably died.

A few of the Westerbork prisoners were deported to Theresienstadt, Bergen-Belsen and Vittel in France. In April 1945, the camp was liberated by Allied troops.

Theresienstadt (Terezin)

The ghetto, originally intended to hold elderly Jews, was established on 24 November 1941 in the former garrison town of Terezin which had been evacuated for this purpose (population approx. 7,000). It is situated about 60 km north of Prague on the flood meadows of the Eger. In fact, Theresienstadt served primarily as a transit camp in the masterplan of the "final solution of the Jewish question" for deportation transports to the extermination camps in the East (Auschwitz and others). The designation "ghetto" served to conceal the true function of the camp. For propaganda reasons, it was sometimes referred to as a *Vorzugslager* (preferential camp) or a *Reichsaltersheim* (Reich retirement home).

The camp initially held Jewish people from Bohemia and Moravia, German Jews over the age of 65 or Jews over 55 in poor health, together with their Jewish spouses and children under 14, war-wounded or decorated Jewish first world war veterans and groups of Jews from Western Europe. Later, in 1943/44, Jews from the ghettos in Eastern Europe and Hungarian camps were also transported to Theresienstadt and, just before the end of the war, prisoners from Eastern concentration camps were also transferred there. More than 152,000 persons entered the camp. In September 1942, the camp held more than 58,000 men, women and children.

Theresienstadt was the responsibility of the *Zentralstelle für jüdische Auswanderung in Prag* ("central office for Jewish emigration in Prague" renamed around 1943 as *Zentralamt für die Regelung der Judenfrage in Böhmen und Mähren* or "central office for the Jewish question in Bohemia and Moravia") which was, in turn, directly answerable to Eichmann's IV B 4 department of the RSHA in Berlin. Many of the camp inmates had been told they were going to a retirement home where they would be cared for in their old age in exchange for giving up their entire property. In reality, conditions at the camp were horrific. The houses and apartments of the town which had previously accommodated a population of 7,000 were now totally overcrowded with tens of thousands of old and sick people, some housed in cellars and attics. The inadequate daily ration (225 g of bread, 60 g of potatoes and a watery soup), lack of water and primitive sanitary conditions did the rest and the mortality rate in the camp was extremely high. An estimated 34,000 people died in Theresienstadt.

From Theresienstadt, people were transported to the extermination camps. Of those who were deported from Theresienstadt, almost 84,000 were killed there. In 1944, a Nazi propaganda film was made at the camp entitled *Der Führer schenkt den Juden eine Stadt* ("The Führer gives the Jews a town"). For the film, and for the benefit of a Danish Red Cross commission, certain cosmetic "improvements" were made to the houses, the ghetto inmates were temporarily given good clothing, and sporting events and musical performances were staged. On 8 May 1945, when Theresienstadt was liberated by Soviet troops, there were still more than 30,000 prisoners in the camp.

Theresienstadt (Terezin) Small Fort	The fortress built at the turn of the 18th century served as a police internment camp. Under the Austro-Hungarian monarchy, the small fortress had been used as a prison for military and civilian prisoners.

In June 1940, the Gestapo headquarters in Prague established a police prison here which soon took on aspects of a concentration camp. Although the small fortress was not actually organisationally linked with the Theresienstadt concentration camp, inmates from the concentration camp were transferred to the small fortress for "special treatment" (a euphemism which invariably meant death); these included, for example, between 30 and 40 children from the ghetto of Białystok, who arrived in Theresienstadt in August 1943 and had fallen ill there. A total of 35,000 prisoners entered the small fortress in the course of the years.

Stutthof (Sztutowo)	The concentration camp of Stutthof was situated 36 km East of Danzig on the outskirts of the village of Stutthof. The camp was initially established in September 1939 as a civilian prison camp and was used from November 1941 onwards as a special SS camp and then from 13 January 1942 as a state concentration camp. The area originally fenced in with barbed-wire ("old camp") was extended in early 1943 by a "new camp" directly adjacent, surrounded by electric fencing, and intended to hold 25,000 prisoners. The "new camp" was never completed. Guards and camp personnel were recruited from the SS.

In early 1942, Stutthof held about 3,000 prisoners. By the end of May 1944, numbers had risen to 8,000. The number of prisoners rose drastically in summer 1944 with the arrival of the Jewish prisoners (including Hungarian Jewish women) and by December 1944/January 1945, together with more than 100 external commandos, the camp counted 52,000 prisoners (of whom more than 33,000 were women). All in all, more than 100,000 prisoners passed through Stutthof, nationals of various European countries (Germans, Poles, Russians, French, Dutch, Belgians, Czechs, Latvians, Lithuanians, Danes, Norwegians, "gypsies"). Some of them were put to work in SS enterprises such as the German armaments works (DAW) which had been set up next to the camp, in brickworks in the surrounding area, in private industrial companies, in agriculture or in the camp workshops.

The mortality rate was high; it was exacerbated by the appalling conditions of work and accommodation and by the completely inadequate nutrition, but above all by the lack of sanitation. A typhoid epidemic in the winter of 1942/43 and a fleck typhus epidemic in the second half of 1944 wiped out a large proportion of the prisoners, and SS medical personnel were forbidden to treat Jewish prisoners. Many prisoners were shot (some of them in the camp's specially equipped execution block or *Genickschussanlage*) or sent to the gas chamber. Many others died of maltreatment. Gassing (with *Zyklon B* cyanide gas) had begun in Stutthof by June 1944 at the latest and was carried out in a gas chamber built in the spring of 1944, which was also used for delousing clothes, as well as in specially sealed railway carriages of a narrow-gauge railway which ran into the camp. Prisoners who fell ill were killed by poison injections at the camp medical station.

In January 1945, the first death-march evacuations from Stutthof began. Many of the exhausted prisoners were shot by the guards because they could no longer walk. Those prisoners who remained in the camp were evacuated by ship in April 1945, some to Flensburg and most of them to Neustätter Bucht. The captains of the *Cap Arcona, Thielbek* and other ships lying at anchor in the Neustätter Bucht, already laden with prisoners from other concentration camps, refused to take any more on board. A number of prisoners succeeded in swimming to the beach, where about 400 of them were shot by the SS. Soviet troops reached the main concentration camp at Stutthof on 1 May 1945, and liberated the remaining 120 prisoners who had been able to hide there.

Kulmhof (Chelmno)

Kulmhof was an extermination camp in the *Reichsgau* of Wartheland. In Kulmhof, a small village near Łódź (Litzmannstadt), an extermination camp was established as part of the "final solution" for Jews who had been transferred from the towns and villages of Wartheland to the Łódź ghetto. It consisted of two sections: the castle, where the killings took place and the *Waldlager* (forest camp) a few kilometers away, where the bodies were buried in mass graves. Kulmhof was equipped and operated by a *Sonderkommando* (special squad). The *Sonderkommando* was divided into three groups: transport, castle and forest squad. The mass murder of Jews began in December 1941 in two and sometimes in three mobile gas chambers or gas-vans.

The transport squad brought the victims by van to the castle. Here, they were told that they were going to be deported to work in the Reich and that they would have to bathe and have their clothes disinfected before they started their journey. After this explanation, the Jews were ordered to undress and hand over their valuables. Polish workers then led them into the cellar of the castle and from there to a side exit, where they were forced into the waiting gas-vans. When the doors were closed, the engine of the van was switched on and the exhaust fumes were piped into the side of the vehicle. The victims were dead in about 10 minutes. The driver then drove off to the *Waldlager* in the forest which was guarded by police on all sides. Jewish workers in chains, some of whom had been temporarily retained from extermination, unloaded the bodies from the gas-van and threw them into ready dug graves. After unloading, the workers cleaned the inside of the gas-van and the mobile gas chamber returned to the castle for further victims. The transports continued until all the Jews who had arrived on any given day in Kulmhof had been killed and brought to the mass graves in the forest. In the summer of 1942, they began opening up the graves to exhume the bodies and burn them. At the end of March 1943, Kulmhof was liquidated. Members of the *Sonderkommando* blew up the castle and shot the Jewish workers. The *Sonderkommando* was transferred to the *Prinz Eugen* Waffen SS Division in Yugoslavia.

In April 1944, the *Sonderkommando* was called back to re-establish the camp. Using the castle cellars which had not been damaged by the blast, some barracks set up in the castle courtyard and in the *Waldlager,* gassing began again. This time, the bodies were burned in the forest in a furnace operated by Jewish slave labourers. In August 1944 work began once again on dissolving the camp. As the Soviet troops closed in, the final order to liquidate the camp came in January 1945. Before the *Sonderkommando* left, the Jewish labourers were killed. They put up considerable resistance. In the first period of the camp, at least 145,000 Jews were killed and in the second period at least 7,176.

Polish estimates put the numbers killed in Kulmhof between 200,000 and 350,000, including about 5,000 Sinti and Roma and 82 children from the Czech village of Lidice.

| Gross-Rosen (Rogoznica) | The concentration camp of Gross-Rosen was established in 1940 as a labour camp near Striegau in the district of Schweidnitz in the former province of Breslau. The camp originally held only a few hundred prisoners, housed in wooden barracks. With the transfer of the arms industry eastwards, Gross-Rosen was constantly enlarged and, on 1 May 1941, it was established as an independent concentration camp. In its final phase, Gross-Rosen had up to 70 satellites or external work squads *(Aussenkommandos)* with a total of some 80,000 prisoners. The main camp itself held about 10,000 prisoners from almost every country in Europe. The inmates were mainly used as slave labour for the German arms industry, but some were also forced to work in stone quarries. |

Brutal and inhuman treatment led to many deaths: prisoners were maltreated by SS men or *Funktionshäftlinge* ("functionary prisoners") and were shot, hanged, drowned or beaten to death on the slightest pretext. Many were killed for allegedly or actually violating penal colony rules or the rules of the *Sonderkommando*.

In early February 1945, Gross-Rosen was evacuated as the front approached; the prisoners were transported in goods wagons or sent on death-marches to other concentration camps within the Reich. On the journey, many died of hunger and exhaustion or were shot. About 20 or 30 prisoners, mainly Russians and Poles, who had hidden in the camp to avoid the evacuation, were discovered and shot by the SS squad who had stayed behind to clear the camp and burn all written documents.

| Majdanek (Lublin-M.) | In October 1941, Majdanek was established as a PoW camp by the Waffen-SS on the south-western outskirts of Lublin on the road to Chelm; it was intended for 25,000 to 50,000 prisoners. Prisoners from Buchenwald, Soviet prisoners of war and Polish civilian workers were used to build the camp. Most of the prisoners were Jewish people from the concentration camps of Theresienstadt, Auschwitz, Sachsenhausen and Dachau and from the Warsaw ghetto. Germans were generally used as *Funktionshäftlinge* ("functionary prisoners"). In the autumn of 1942, an open women's division was established for Polish women and girls who had been imprisoned on "political grounds". Unauthorised secondary school attendance (only primary school attendance was permitted) was, for example, adequate reason for imprisonment. |

The prisoners were made to undertake various kinds of work in agriculture, forestry and other areas (ten satellites). Clothing, nutrition, accommodation and sanitary conditions in the camp were utterly inadequate. Many prisoners died of disease, starvation or exhaustion, were beaten to death, shot "attempting to escape" (for which the sharpshooter was granted special leave), hanged or put to death in other ways. Prisoners with infectious diseases or suspected of carrying infectious diseases (typhus) were "selected" on the orders of the RSHA and shot.

By October 1942 at the latest, a gas chamber was in operation in the camp. It initially consisted of two gas chambers in a wooden barracks. Later, further gas chambers were set up in a stone building. According to court findings, Majdanek had "at least 3 concrete-built chambers with sealed steel doors". Transports of Jews from Germany, the Netherlands, Italy and other countries were selected on arrival at the camp and prisoners deemed fit for work were allocated to labour squads. Persons deemed unfit for work (women, children and the elderly) were then killed either by *Zyklon B* (cyanide gas pellets) or carbon monoxide. Prisoners who became ill and unable to work were "selected" periodically and gassed. In May 1943, several hundred Jewish children met their deaths in the gas chambers. According to court investigations, an estimated 200,000 persons were gassed in Majdanek up to the autumn of 1943.

In April 1944, the evacuation of Majdanek began. The last death-march from the camp began just before the liberation of Lublin by Soviet troops on 22nd July 1944.

Treblinka	An extermination camp to the north of Warsaw on the Warsaw-Białystok railway line. The construction of Treblinka II began in late May/early June 1942 under the command of the SS central construction department of the chief of police and SS in Warsaw. In addition to Poles, the work force also consisted of Jews interned in the adjacent labour camp of Treblinka I.

On completion, the camp had three sections: the accommodation block (SS accommodation, administrative buildings, barracks for Polish, Ukrainian workers and Jewish prisoners, stalls, zoo and so on), the arrival block for incoming Jews (including the railway ramp, square, barracks for storing property confiscated from the Jews, barracks for undressing, selection square, "hospital") and the so-called upper camp or death camp (gas chambers, pits, accommodation für the Jewish *Sonderkommando* and later crematoria). The camp staff was made up of about 40 German and 120 Ukrainian volunteers. The latter were mainly on guard duty, but were also employed in the mass murder of the Jews.

In July 1942, the camp was "ready for operation". Since 23 July 1942, transports of Jews had been arriving continuously, especially from Warsaw and the surrounding district. The extermination procedure was similar to that in Bełzec and Sobibór: on arrival, the Jews were devided into men, women and children. They were told they were to be deported to labour camps and that they had to bathe, hand over their clothing and luggage for disinfection and deposit any gold, money, foreign currency or jewellery with the cashier for reasons of safety. Women and children were then brought into one barracks where they had to undress for "showers". The men waited in front of the barracks while the women and children were driven through a small alley to the death camp and into the gas chambers by German and Ukrainian camp personnel wielding sticks, whips or rifles. After the women and children had been gassed and the gas chambers had been cleared out, the men, who had by now undressed, were also driven into the death camp, where they were either gassed or shot on the edge of specially dug pits.

From time to time, the SS selected men who were fit for work and, less often, women, for camp work squads. Gassing by means of vehicle exhaust fumes took place in three small gas-chambers; in September 1942 the capacity was considerably increased by building larger chambers. The bodies were thrown into pits. Shortly before the liquidation of the camp, the bodies of those who had been murdered were exhumed and burned in the open air along with more recent victims.

A rebellion by prisoners on 2 August 1943 accelerated the liquidation of the camp. The buildings were demolished and the entire site was levelled. At the end of November 1943, the camp was dissolved. At least 700,000 Jews were killed in Treblinka.

Bełzec	Construction work on the Bełzec extermination camp at the south-eastern border of the Lublin district of the *Generalgouvernement* began in the late autumn of 1941. Bełzec was completed in early March 1942. Gassing was initially carried out in a wooden barracks lined with sheet metal, with a capacity of 100 to 150 persons. Later, the SS erected a stone building with six gas chambers which could hold about 1,500 persons. After initial experiments with bottled gas, it was finally decided, on economic grounds, to use the exhaust fumes from tank or truck engines to kill the victims.

The camp was staffed by former "euthanasia" workers, SS men and police. The guards were Ukrainian volunteers and *Volksdeutsche* (ethnic Germans).

On the arrival of "transfer trains" in Bełzec, the Jewish men and then the Jewish women and children were sent to the gas chambers, which were fitted out to look like showers. The gassing took about 10 minutes. After airing the gas chambers, they were cleared out by the *Arbeitsjuden* ("work Jews"). Before the bodies were thrown into the mass graves standing ready nearby, special prisoner squads searched them to locate any valuables (gold teeth, rings). In early December 1942, the SS stopped exterminations. Until March 1943, the bodies were exhumed and burned and then the camp was liquidated.

At least 400,000 Jews were murdered in Bełzec. The actual number of victims, however, is probably well over 600,000.

Sobibór
For the extermination camp of Sobibór, a wooded site in a sparsely populated area on the eastern border of the Lublin district was chosen.

After completing the main construction work, a "trial gassing" of 30 or 40 Jewish women was carried out in the *Vergasungsanstalt* (gassing unit) which consisted of three chambers with a capacity of between 150 and 200 each. The victims were killed by the exhaust fumes of a tank or vehicle engine channelled into the gas chambers.

Mass killings began in May 1942. After unloading at the railway station of Sobibór, the Jews were brought into the camp, given a reassuring speech and instructed to undress for bathing and to hand over their valuables. They were then driven in groups into the gas chambers which were located in a secluded part of the camp. After gassing, the bodies were buried in mass graves by a Jewish work squad. When transport difficulties occurred in July 1942, the opportunity was used to expand the capacity of the gas chambers.

In the autumn of 1942, the SS began covering up the traces of mass murder. The bodies of the victims were exhumed and burned in pires in a pit. The bodies of more recent victims were transported from the gas chambers direct to the pires by the *Leichenkommando* (body squad).

On 14 October 1943, Jewish prisoners rebelled against the SS and an unknown number of them managed to escape; those who remained were shot and the camp was liquidated.

In Sobibór, the murder victims were Jews from the ghettos of the *Generalgouvernement,* the Reich (including Austria), the *Protektorat,* Slovakia, Holland and France. It is no longer possible to determine the precise number of victims.

Documentary material indicates that no fewer than 150,000 Jews were killed at Sobibór. According to Polish sources based on statements by Polish railway officials regarding the number of transports into the camp, the number of victims at Sobibór was in the region of 250,000, not counting those brought in for extermination on foot, by horse-drawn cart or by truck.

Auschwitz (Oświęcim)
The largest of all the concentration and extermination camps was built near the town of Oświęcim (Auschwitz) in the industrial heartland of Upper Silesia. It was divided into three main camp areas: Auschwitz I (the *Stammlager* or "old camp"), Auschwitz II (Birkenau) and Auschwitz III (Monowitz).

Auschwitz I was established in May/July 1940 in a former Austrian artillery barracks and was initially used mainly for the internment of political prisoners (members of the resistance and Polish intellectuals). Until 1943, the number of prisoners in the *Stammlager* of Auschwitz I rose to about 30,000. The *Stammlager* consisted of the internment camp with prisoners' accommodation blocks and the external premises of the commanding officers. The actual internment camp area was surrounded by a four-metre-high barbed wire perimeter fence, which was under high voltage current at night. There were watchtowers along the length of the perimeter fence.

Auschwitz II (Birkenau) was established in late 1941, early 1942 about 3 km from the *Stammlager* and was continuously expanded right up to the end of the war. The camp covers a total area of some 175 hectares with more than 250 stone buildings and wooden barracks and several camp sections separated by barbed-wire fences. Men and women were kept separate. New arrivals deemed fit for work were first quarantined and then distributed throughout the camp. In September 1943, when whole families of Czech Jews were brought to Auschwitz from Theresienstadt, the so-called Czech Family Camp (also known as the Theresienstadt Camp) was established. Jews from this camp who were deemed fit to work were then transferred to the other camps and the others were gassed in the camp in March and July 1944. A further partial camp was the Gypsy Camp. At the west side of the grounds was the store, referred to within the camp as "Canada", where the luggage, clothing, jewellery, watches and other belongings taken from the Jews were stored and sorted. Birkenau was surrounded by a high double barbed-wire fence, which was electrified at night, as were the barbed-wire fences of the individual camp sections. Some 150,000 prisoners were held in the camp as a whole.

Auschwitz III, Monowitz, was set up in 1941 to serve the IG Farben company, which had a production works (Buna-Werk) on the site. Monowitz was the largest of the 40 or so satellites to be established in the Upper Silesian industrial area. In November 1943, the camps of Birkenau and Monowitz were put under separate adminstration and were each allocated a commandant of their own. The political department, the medical officer and the telegraphic station remained in the *Stammlager* of Auschwitz I.

Conditions for prisoners in Auschwitz were inhuman. Prisoners slept in unheated stone buildings or barracks on three-tiered wooden bunks with only straw or wood shavings, three or even four prisoners to each bunk, mostly without sheets and with one small blanket to cover them. The wood shavings and the straw were crawling with vermin. Sanitary and hygienic conditions were entirely inadequate. Given the number of diarrhoeic illnesses, there were far too few latrines, and in Birkenau all the wells were contaminated with coli bacteria.

Apart from the IG Farben company, the prisoners also worked in SS-operated production works (armaments, stone quarries) and for other industrial enterprises in the Upper Silesian area. Malnutrition, exhaustion, illness and epidemics (typhus, dysentery, cholera) led to mass deaths amongst prisoners. Maltreatment and arbitrary killings further increased the mortality rate.

Many medical experiments were carried out on prisoners in Auschwitz (experiments on twins, sterilisation and other "research").

In early September 1941, the first killings of prisoners using *Zyklon B* cyanide gas began in the camp. Gassing was carried out in the detention cells of Block 11 of the Auschwitz I *Stammlager*. However, as the cells were so small, a gas chamber was soon built in the crematorium of the *Stammlager*. It was used for the first time to gas a shipment of 900 Russian prisoners. From October 1941 onwards, small groups of Jews were also killed in this gas chamber.

In January 1942, a farmhouse in Auschwitz II (Birkenau) was converted into a gas chamber. It was initially used to kill Jews from Upper Silesia. Deportation transports followed from all the German-occupied countries of Europe. All the people who arrived on the first transport were killed without exception. Soon afterwards, however, "selections" were introduced and these were carried out immediately on arrival of the trainloads of Jews on the ramp at Birkenau. The "selections" meant that those deemed fit for work (on average 10 to 15 percent of any one transport) were allocated forced labour and the others were sent directly to the gas chambers.

As the deportations increased, a further farmhouse in Birkenau was converted to a gas chamber in June 1942. Later, to expand the killing capacity at Birkenau, two large and two smaller crematoriums with gas chambers were also built. The larger crematoria (crematorium 2 and crematorium 3), each with a capacity of 3,000 persons per gas chamber, went into operation in the spring of 1943. Not only the men, women and children on the incoming transports who were unfit for work were sent to the gas chambers on arrival; sick and unfit prisoners were "selected" from time to time in the *Stammlager* and the satellite camps and either killed in the gas chambers or in the medical station by injections of phenol (carbolic acid).

From late October/early November 1944 the gas chambers in the camp were destroyed (the last was destroyed in January 1945 shortly before Soviet troops arrived). It is not known exactly how many people were killed in Auschwitz, as prisoners destined for the gas chambers were not given a registration number. Estimates put the figure at between 1 and 1.5 million. Camp commandant Höss initially quoted 2.5 million gassed prisoners and half a million deaths through illness, but later revised the number of deaths to a total of 1.3 million.

Mittelbau-Dora

Mittelbau-Dora was a concentration camp and subterranean armaments centre near Nordhausen in the Southern Harz mountains. Following a bombing raid on the rocket test station of Peenemünde on 17/18 August 1943, the secret project to build the V2 rocket was continued in bomb-proof shafts and caverns. On 28 August 1943 the first prisoners arrived from Buchenwald to work in the *Dora* squad in Mittelbau. Work began on creating a system of tunnels in the mountain of Berg Kohnstein.

By the end of the year, the number of prisoners had risen to almost 11,000. The prisoners were subjected to extremely demanding physical work. Masses of stone and tons of machinery were moved by human power alone. The prisoners' accommodation was catastrophic. In the early period, there were no barracks at all. The prisoners remained in the dark and dusty caverns day and night. There were no washing facilities, nutrition was poor and the prisoners were constantly subject to SS terror. Mortality was extremely high.

Once V2 production had begun and the barracks were completed in the summer of 1944, conditions for the prisoners were "normalised". Up to 14,500 prisoners worked underground in the mountain caverns at any one time. In March 1945, the camp held more than 40,000 prisoners, partly as a result of evacuations from concentration camps further east. Almost 6,000 V2 rockets were produced in Mittelbau-Dora, where some 60,000 prisoners (from 20 different countries) were set to work, of whom at least 20,000 died.

In early April, the evacuation transports and death marches began to Ravensbrück and Bergen-Belsen. On 11 April 1945, American troops reached the camp.

Bergen-Belsen

The concentration camp near Celle in northern Germany (in operation from March 1943) was completed in mid July 1943. It was intended for the internment of approximately 10,000 female and male Jewish prisoners of various European nationalities, who had been promised emigration in exchange for ethnic German immigrants. At first, the inmates were not set to work, and it was only from 1944 onwards that forced labour was introduced for some of the prisoners. Bergen-Belsen was divided into a number of separate sections, the largest of which was the *Sternlager* (Star of David Camp). The second largest was the so-called *Neutralenlager* (Neutrals Camp) for Jews from neutral states. Standards of nutrition, accommodation and hygiene were comparable to the appalling conditions that prevailed in all the concentration camps. Although Bergen-Belsen was supposedly a "preferential camp" the prisoners were maltreated and beaten by the *Blockälteste* and the heads of the work squads.

Some exchanges were carried out in 1944, allowing emigration to Palestine (222 persons) in exchange for German citizens imprisoned there, to Switzerland (1,685 Hungarian Jews) for a per capita payment of approximately $ 1,000 and to the USA and North Africa (approximately 800 persons) in exchange for German citizens imprisoned in America. In the course of 1943, sick prisoners from other concentration camps were allocated to a special section (*Erholungslager* or "convalescent camp") where some 2,000 prisoners were held. Lack of medication and miserable hygienic conditions led to many deaths. Particularly in June/July 1944, many seriously ill prisoners were killed by injections of phenol (carbolic acid). In addition to the *Erholungslager*, an "admissions camp" was established for Polish women in mid-August, which was totally overcrowded towards the end of 1944 and the beginning of 1945 with thousands of sick female prisoners from Auschwitz (amongst them Anne Frank). Towards the end of the war, Bergen-Belsen was used as a transit camp for thousands of prisoners evacuated from other concentration camps. Catastrophe struck: from February 1944 onwards, new arrivals were not even registered. The death toll through starvation, epidemics and exhaustion was vast. Between early January 1945 and the middle of April 1945 alone, some 35,000 people died in Bergen-Belsen.

On 15 April 1945, British troops arrived in Bergen-Belsen. At the time, there were some 60,000 survivors in the camp, of whom 13,000 succumbed to exhaustion or illness even after their liberation. A total of some 50,000 concentration camp prisoners and between 30,000 and 50,000 PoWs died in Bergen-Belsen. Today, on the site of the concentration camp, there are huge mass graves.

Notes

1   Primo Levi, The Drowned and the Saved, London 1989, pp. 93–94.

2   Reinhard Kühn, Konzentrationslagen Sachsenhausen, issued by the Landeszentrale für politische Bildungsarbeit Berlin, 2nd edition, Berlin 1990, p.17.

3   As early as the 1920s, Carl Schmitt's theory of statecraft outlines in theory what would later come into effect in the concentration camps. "The essential political distinction is the distinction between friend and foe" writes Schmitt. (Der Begriff des Politischen, first published in 1927, 3rd edition, Hamburg 1933, p.7). The friend-foe relationship, however, cannot be derived from any prescribed norm; it is a question of sovereign decision-making. Whenever one calls upon standards which are considered necessary and universal, irrespective of whether they are based on faith, natural law, declarations of human rights or proclamations of civil rights or concepts for a good and just society, there can be no real decision-making any more because one has renounced that right and subjected one's own power to the standards. This is why one must liberate oneself from all that is normative as from fetters and this is consistent with one of Carl Schmitt's key maxims: "The decision, in normative terms, is born of nothing!" (Politische Theologie, Munich 1922, p.31). Another is: "The best thing in the world is an order!" (Legalität und Legitimität, Munich 1932, p.13).

4   Cited in Ursachen und Folgen. Vom deutschen Zusammenbruch 1918 und 1945 bis zur staatlichen Neuordnung Deutschlands in der Gegenwart. A collection of records and documents on German history from 1918 onwards, edited by Herbert Michaelis and Ernst Schraepler, vol. IX, Berlin 1964, p.74. The Göring quote which follows is from p.38 of the same source.

5   Kommandant in Auschwitz. The memoirs of Rudolf Höss, edited by Martin Broszat, 13th edition, paperback, Munich 1992, p.66.

6   Eugen Kogon, Der SS-Staat – Das System der Deutschen Konzentrationslager, Munich 1974, p.51. English title: The Theory and Practice of Hell, New York 1956 (o/p).

7   The political prisoners who survived thanks to being given long prison sentences included Erich Honecker, who later became Secretary General of the SED and Chairman of the State Council of the GDR. The resistance fighters arrested following the unsuccessful attempt to assassinate Adolf Hitler were subject to interrogation and torture by the Gestapo. Nevertheless, as they were sentenced by the Volksgerichtshof (People's Court of Justice) in show trials, they were imprisoned in Berlin's Moabit gaol, where the prison guards treated them with respect, allowing them to write letters or reports for the prison chaplain.

8   Die Ordnung des Terrors: Das Konzentrationslager, Frankfurt am Main 1993, p.220.

9   Ibid., p.193 f.

10 Kommandant in Auschwitz, op.cit., p. 172 f.

11 Rainer Eisfeld, Die unmenschliche Fabrik: V2 Produktion und KZ 'Mittelbau-Dora', Erfurt, undated, p.37.

12 Soziologie des Kommunismus, Cologne and Berlin 1952, p.356.

13 The Drowned and the Saved, op.cit., p. 96.

14 In spite of the similarities invoked between the old and new state on the Day of Potsdam, 21 March 1993, Hitler never took any interest in Prussian history, never visited the royal residence of Sanssouci and never named any SS Division after a Prussian king or general in World War II. The last Prussian Day in German history may be regarded as 20 July 1944, the day of the failed assassination attempt against Hitler, which involved so many traditional Prussian names. Admittedly, this date also indicates the extent of the dissolution of Prussia's power: only a small minority felt any commitment to the Prussian tradition of rebellion against injustice and violence.

15 Eugen Kogon, born in 1903, was arrested in 1938 and imprisoned in Buchenwald from 1939 until

the end of the war. In 1945, he wrote a report for an intelligence team of the American Psychological Warfare Division, which was subsequently edited and published in book form in 1946 under the title Der SS-Staat – Das System der Konzentrationslager (English title: The Theory and Practice of Hell).

16 An address by Reichsführer SS Heinrich Himmler on 4 October 1943 to leading SS officers in Poznan: from the records of the Nuremberg Trials. [Translator's note: Himmler speech, 4 October 1943; International Military Tribunal, Nuremberg, document PS 1919. The English version quoted here was cited in: Martin Gilbert, The Holocaust; The Jewish Tragedy, London 1986].

17 Kommandant in Auschwitz, op.cit., p.168 f.

18 Wolfgang Sofsky, Die Ordnung des Terrors, op.cit., p.186

19 Kommandant in Auschwitz, op.cit., p.134 f.

20 Auschwitz in den Augen der SS (Auschwitz through the eyes of the the SS), State Auschwitz Museum, Warsaw 1992, p.15.

21 Ibid., p.156 ff.

22 Primo Levi, If This Is a Man, London 1979, p.48.

23 Primo Levi, The Drowned and the Saved, op.cit., p.63.

24 Wolfgang Sofsky, Die Ordnung des Terrors, op.cit., p.160.

25 Sofsky, op.cit., p.162.

26 Primo Levi, If This Is a Man, op.cit., p.95 f.

27 Ibid., p.96.

28 J.Mostowski, in: Z.Ryn / S. Klodzinski, An der Grenze zwischen Leben und Tod - eine Studie über die Erscheinung des 'Muselmanns' im Konzentrationslager; Auschwitz Hefte I, Weinheim and Basel 1987, p.128 f.
[Translator's note: In a footnote on p.94 of If This is a Man Primo Levi comments "The word Muselmann, I do not know why, was used by the old ones of the camp to describe the weak, the inept, those doomed to selection. When a group of these emaciated figures, crushed to the ground, was viewed from a distance, they resembled Muslims at prayer – which is probably the source of the term Muselmann that was given to the starving prisoners. They were completely apathetic to their surroundings and were no longer able to function – not even to commit suicide."]

29 Hitlers Herrschaft – Vollzug einer Weltanschauung 2nd edition Stuttgart 1988, p.133 f.

30 A joke once popular in Zionist circles in Palestine, macabre as it may seem in retrospect, gives an insight: A Jew arriving after 1933, is asked on immigration "Kommen Sie aus Überzeugung?" ("Have you come here out of personal conviction?") and replies, "Nein, aus Deutschland." ("No, out of Germany.")

31 The motive of enrichment in one sense or another tended to play a more important role amongst those who denounced others as alleged "enemies of the people" in order to have them sent to a concentration camp. They hoped, for example, to be able to take over the victim's apartment or to get an irritating colleague or rival shopkeeper out of the way. However, one cannot use such opportunism alone as an explanation for the establishment of the concentration camps in the first place.

32 Some light can be shed on the ruling system in the Third Reich by an obscure and thought-provoking chapter written more than one hundred years before by Hegel in his Phänomenologie des Geistes (Phenomenology of Mind) under the title Herrschaft und Knechtschaft (Power and Servitude). Put simply, this chapter states that the master gains his self-esteem from his power over "the others" who live in fear of the master; their obedience is the stuff of which his pride and his sense of honour are made. The servant, on the other hand, gains his self-esteem through the act of self-denial and transference: he identifies with the master. The stronger and less doubted the master, the stronger the power which binds the servant in his reflected glory or image. Could this give us an insight into the excesses of the Hitler cult? It should be added that the servants themselves also need people to whom they can pass on their own subjugation and self-denial. In this respect, Sofsky has stated: "The face of modern systematic terror is not shaped by the all-powerful, invulnerable masters, but by the excesses of the underlings of power."(Die Ordnung des Terrors, op. cit., p.318).

33 See Die Deutschen in ihrem Jahrhundert 1890-1990, Reinbek 1990, by the author of this publication.

34 See Die Deutschen vor ihrer Zukunft, Berlin 1993, by the author of this publication.

35 Politische Ethik und Christentum, Göttingen 1904, p.6.

36 Although the international economic crisis did, of course, act as a catalyst, it also hit other countries, particularly Britain and the USA, without comparable repercussions, let alone the destruction of the political system.

37 Mein Kampf, 190th-194th edition, Munich 1936, p. 129.

38 Sofsky, Die Ordnung des Terrors, op.cit., p.20.

39 Cited in: Renzo Vespignani, Faschismus, 5th edition, Berlin 1979, p.87.

40 Moabiter Sonette, Berlin 1946; see also the collection of German political poems published under the title Deutschland, Deutschland – Politische Gedichte vom Vormärz bis zur Gegenwart, edited by Helmut Lamprecht, Bremen 1969, p.441 f – Albrecht Haushofer was murdered by the Gestapo in Berlin-Moabit on 23 April 1945.

306

Bibliography   *The following is a necessarily subjective selection of some important publications on the German concentration camps. As it is by no means exhaustive, it should be regarded merely as a guideline for further reading.*

Adler, H.G., Theresienstadt 1941-1945. Das Antlitz einer Zwangsgemeinschaft, Tübingen 1960.

Adler, H.G., Der verwaltete Mensch. Studien zur Deportation der Juden aus Deutschland, Tübingen 1974.

Antoni E., KZ – Von Dachau bis Auschwitz. Faschistische Konzentrationslager 1933-1945, Frankfurt am Main 1979.

Arendt, H., Eichmann in Jerusalem. A Report of the Banality of Evil, London 1977.

Aronson, S., The Beginnings of the Gestapo System, Jerusalem 1969.

Ball-Kaduri, K.J. Vor der Katastrophe. Juden in Deutschland 1934-1939, Tel Aviv 1967.

Bettelheim, B., Individual and Mass Behaviour in Extreme Situations, Irvington 1993.

Broszat, M. et al., The Hitler State: The Foundation and Development of the Internal Structure of the Third Reich, London 1981.

Crankshaw, E., Gestapo: Instrument of Tyranny, London 1990.

Czech, D., Auschwitz Chronicle 1939-1945, London 1990.

Deschner, Günther, Reinhard Heydrich. Statthalter der totalen Macht, Esslingen 1977.

Ferber, W., 55 Monate Dachau. Ein Tatsachenbericht, Bremen 1993.

Fraenkel, E., Dual State, Hippocrene Books, 1941/1969.

Fraenkel, H./Manvell, R., Himmler. Kleinbürger und Massenmörder, Berlin/Frankfurt am Main/Vienna, 1965.

Georg, E. Die wirtschaftlichen Unternehmungen der SS, Stuttgart 1963.

Gilbert, M., Atlas of the Holocaust, New York 1993.

Graml, H., Reichskristallnacht. Antisemitismus und Judenverfolgung im Dritten Reich, Munich 1988.

Grosser, A., Ermordung der Menschheit. Der Genozid im Gedächtnis der Völker, Munich/Vienna 1990.

Henkys, R., Die nationalsozialistische Gewaltverbrechen. Geschichte und Gericht. Stuttgart/Berlin 1964.

Hilberg, R., The Destruction of the European Jews, New York/London 1985.

Himmler, H., Geheimreden 1993 bis 1945 und andere Ansprachen, edited by B.F. Smith and A.F. Petersen, Frankfurt am Main/Berlin/Vienna, 1974.

Höhne, H., der Orden unter dem Totenkopf. Die Geschichte der SS.

Höss, R., Kommandant in Auschwitz, edited by M.Broszat, Stuttgart 1958 (republished Munich 1992). English: Commandant of Auschwitz: The Autobiography of Rudolf Höss, London, 1961.

Jäckel, E./Rohwer, J. (eds.) Der Mord an den Juden im Zweiten Weltkrieg. Entschlussbildung und Verwirklichung, Frankfurt am Main 1987.

Jäckel, E., Hitler's World View: A Blueprint for Power, (HUD) 1981.

Jäckel, E., Hitler in History, Tauber/U Pr, 1984.

Jäger, H., Verbrechen unter totalitärer Herrschaft. Studien zur Nationalsozialistischen Gewaltkriminalität, Frankfurt am Main, 1982.

Kaienbrug, H., "Vernichtung durch Arbeit". Der Fall Neuengamme. Die Wirtschaftsbestrebungen der SS und ihre Auswirkungen auf die Existenzbedingungen der KZ-Gefangenen, Bonn 1991.

Kielar, W., Anus Mundi. Fünf Jahre Auschwitz, Frankfurt am Main 1982.

Kirstein, W., Das Konzentrationslager als Institution des totalen Terrors. Das Beispiel KL Natzweiler, Pfaffenweiler 1992.

Klee, E., "Euthanasie" im NS-Staat. Die "Vernichtung lebensunwerten Lebens", Frankfurt am Main 1983.

Klee, F./Dressen, W. (eds.), "Gott mit uns" – der Deutsche Vernichtungskrieg im Osten 1939-1945, Frankfurt am Main 1989.

Kogon, E., Der SS-Staat. Das System der deutschen Konzentrationslager, Munich 1974.

Kogon, E.,/Langbein, H.,/Rückerl, A. et al. (eds.), Nazi Mass Murder by Poison Gas. (trans. M.Scott and C.Lloyd-Morris), New York/London 1994.

Kolb, E., Bergen-Belsen 1943–1945, Göttingen 1985.

Krausnik H./Wilhelm, H.H., Die Truppe des Weltanschauungskrieges. Die Einsatzgruppen der Sicherheitspolizei und des SD 1938-1942, Stuttgart 1981.

Langbein, H., Der Auschwitz-Prozess. Eine Dokumentation. Vienna 1965.

Lanzmann, C., Shoah. An Oral History of the Holocaust, New York 1985.

Lauber, H., Judenpogrom. "Reichskristallnacht" November 1938 in Grossdeutschland. Daten, Fakten, Dokumente, Quellentexte, Thesen und Bewertungen, Gerlingen 1981.

Levi, P., If This is a Man (trans. Stuart Woolf), London 1960.

Levi, P., The Drowned and the Saved (trans. R.Rosenthal), New York 1988/London 1989.

Lichtenstein H., Majdanek. Reportage eine Prozesses, Frankfurt am Main 1979.

Longerich, P. (ed.) Die Ermordung der europäischen Juden, Munich 1989.

Matussek, Die Konzentrationslagerhaft und ihre Folgen, Berlin 1971.

Naujoks, H., Mein Leben im KZ Sachsenhausen 1936–1942. Erinnerung des ehemaligen Lagerältesten, Cologne 1987.

Pingel, E., Häftlinge unter SS Herrschaft. Widerstand, Selbstbehauptung und Vernichtung in Konzentrationslagern, Hamburg 1978.

Pollak, M., Die Grenzen des Sagbaren. Lebensgeschichten von KZ-Häftlingen als Augenzeugenberichte und Identitätsarbeit, Frankfurt am Main/New York 1988.

Rashke, R., Escape from Sobibor, Boston 1982.

Reichmann, E.G., Die Flucht in den Hass. Die Ursachen der deutschen Judenkatastrophe, Frankfurt am Main 1956.

Reitlinger, G., The Final Solution: The Attempt to Exterminate the Jews of Europe 1939-1945. London 1953/1987.

Rose, R./Weiss, W., Sinti und Roma in "Dritten Reich". Das Programm der Vernichtung durch Arbeit, Göttingen 1991.

Rosh, L./Jäckel, E., "Der Tod ist ein Meister aus Deutschland". Deportation und Ermordung der Juden. Kollaboration und Verweigerung in Europa, Hamburg 1990.

Rovan, J., Geschichten aus Dachau, Stuttgart 1989.

Schnabel, R., Macht ohne Moral. Eine Dokumentation über die SS, Frankfurt am Main 1957.

Schwarz, G., Die nationalsozialistischen Lager, Frankfurt am Main/New York 1990.

Segev, T., Soldiers of Evil: The Commandants of the Nazi Concentration Camps, (trans. H.Walzman), New York 1988/London 1990.